CW00869113

An Anthology of

Hampshire Churches

Sketches of a Lifetime

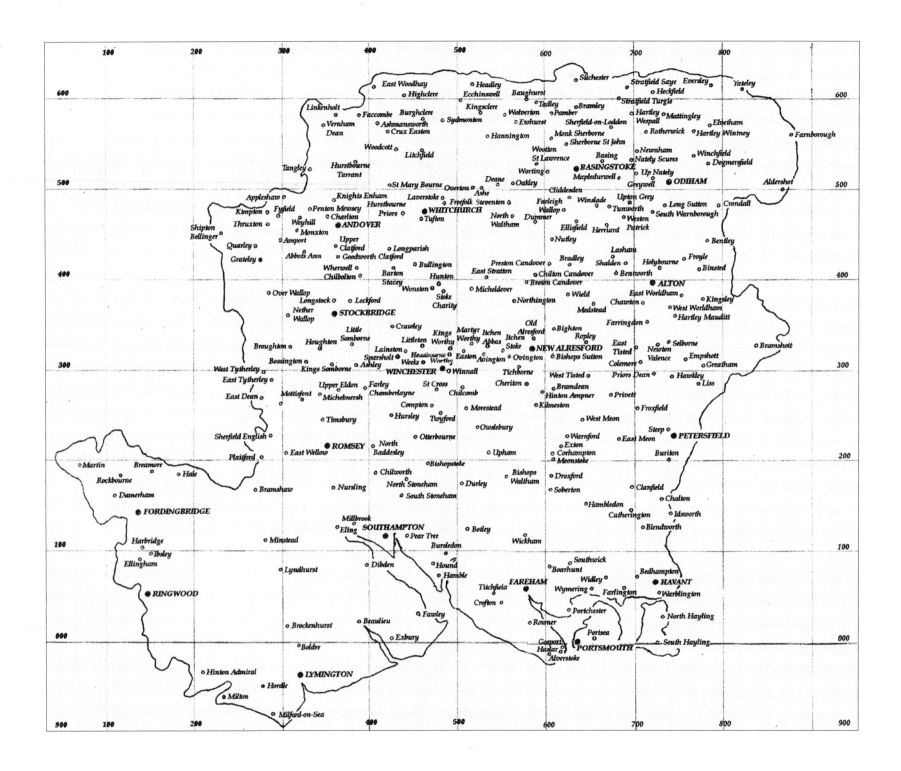

An Anthology of

Hampshire Churches

Sketches of a Lifetime

Anthony New

Phillimore Book Publishing

2018

Published by

PHILLIMORE BOOK PUBLISHING

www.phillimorebookpublishing.co.uk

© Anthony New, 2018

ISBN 978-0-9934680-7-0

CONTENTS

FEATURES TO LOOK FOR IN AN OLD ENGLISH CHURCH

Spire-light
Spire
Broach
Belfry
Transom
Louvres
Wall-arcade
Bosses
Niche
Corbel
Clerestory
Finial
Bell-cote
Sanctus Bell
Cinquefoil Window
Rectangular Buttresses
Lancet Window
Royal Arms
Tower Arch
North Arcade
Chancel Arch
Hatchment
Respond
Capital
Font
Stoup
Parclose Screen
Pampet
Battlements
Crocketed Pinnacle
Balusters
Cornice
Keystone
Base
NAVE
NORTH AISLE
Pulpit
Lectern
Gargoyle
Wall-tablet
Easter Sepulchre
Diagonal Buttress
Aumbry
Impost
Pilaster
S. AISLE
Hagioscope or Squint
CHANCEL
High Altar
Sanctuary
South Porch (17th century)
Pediment
Rood Loft Stair
Apse
Barge Board
Tympanum
Churchyard Cross
Headstones
Table Tomb
Vestry or Sacristy
Altar Rails
Sedilia
Piscina
Plinth
Crypt or Undercroft

A | S | B
N | E | W
1965

DETAILS OF A WINDOW

Three-light window with Bar Tracery
Cusp
Dripstone or Label or Hood Mould
Quatrefoil
Trefoil
Label Stop
Uncusped Head
Jamb
Mullion
Ashlar
Cill or Sill
Diamond Panes with Lead Canes

PREFACE

This series of pictures results from a 76-year period of visiting, sketching and photographing ancient churches, but the idea of collecting together all those of Hampshire is relatively recent and springs from persuasion by my family, who have made many helpful suggestions. They envisaged it as a progression over the years from 'schoolboy' sketches to those showing some results from my architectural training. However that would have produced an apparently random sequence, and I've favoured a straightforward alphabetical layout for ease of reference, with the admitted disadvantage that adjoining entries will usually be unrelated.

The technique and quality of the drawings have obviously varied over the years, and they mostly fall into fairly distinct periods – first when I lived in Hertfordshire as a student and ventured further south by bicycle, secondly when I was stationed at the Royal Navy Signal School at Leydene near East Meon, thirdly when a little house in Winchester, used by my daughter as a student herself, formed a base for cycling or motoring expeditions, and finally in the last two decades when actually living in the county. The earlier sketches have much more sentimental value than artistic and I should perhaps explain my influences.

The starting point was an aversion to games at Highgate School, which at the outset of World War II was evacuated to North Devon. Allowable alternatives to cricket, football or running were either gardening or the school Archaeological Society, run by one of the masters, Dr R.D. Reid. That appealed to me because it involved cycling to local buildings of interest (mostly churches) and in due course producing a little guide book which was printed locally. It seemed to me that the physical exercise was thus put to better use than on the games field, in spite of dauntingly steep hills in every direction, and I was lucky to have encouragement of that kind. The school then had no art department, but I was allowed to enrol part-time at the small Art School in Bideford (three hilly miles each way) and certainly benefited from the expertise there.

The other strong influence was my uncle Edmund Hort New. He had died some years before my days in Devon, but he spent his life (mostly in Oxford) producing drawings for book illustrations, framed pictures, book-plates and the like – all in black-and-white for he was colour-blind. As I write I have a big framed print beside me with his detailed panorama of Florence, every important building being annotated in the margin. I also have the original, bigger similar drawing of 'The City and Port of London' which was included in one of the Royal Academy summer exhibitions in the 1920s. I was only seven when he died, but his painstaking work has always been familiar from such pictures.

Naturally I was guided towards the architectural profession, even at that critical time in the war when the school had few resources for giving such advice, and the Armed Services were beckoning. My parents were augmenting a meagre income by taking in a lodger, an architect's son who was a student at an architectural school, and so it was that I started a five-year course myself at the Northern Polytechnic in Holloway Road, London in the autumn of 1941.

Early in 1945, with the war nearing its climax, I was called to the Navy and after a spell at Leydene near Petersfield (with interesting churches all around) was eventually based in a drawing office on the outskirts of Plymouth with the task of producing large-scale drawings of radio circuits for tuition purposes. Towards the end of 1947 I was able to resume architectural studies where I had left off, and in four years became a junior assistant in a London practice dealing with war damage repairs.

After a couple of changes I applied for a post as senior assistant to Lord Mottistone, then Surveyor to St Paul's Cathedral, and to my surprise and joy was accepted in his well-known firm of Seely and Paget which, unknown to me then, had designed Petersfield Town Hall many years before. My job entailed work not only in connection with St Paul's, but also war damage repairs to many London churches and other historic buildings, as well as new churches and their ancillaries in other parts of the country. It also led to the development of a scheme for completing Portsmouth Cathedral, which for various reasons had to be abandoned for many years until what we see today was achieved in a different form. So the journey to Hampshire and the Isle of Wight became very familiar. After Lord Mottistone's death in 1963 much of his work was taken over by Paul Paget. John Betjeman, their neighbour in the London office, was a like-minded close friend to both, and when Paul's secretary Elizabeth and I became engaged he took a kindly interest and gave us several books that we now treasure. His *Collins Guide to English Parish Churches* has been well-thumbed ever since and was invaluable in checking many of the noteworthy items in the text of this book.

After a period as sole practitioner, during which I was architect to Derby Cathedral and continued to work for many of the London churches and for the Roman Catholic diocese of Northampton, I was able to relinquish those responsibilities gradually, but still to take an active interest in drawing and photography.

My criterion for inclusion of the churches is that they were founded for parish use not later than 1800. So 'Victorian' buildings are excluded, except in the many instances where they have replaced earlier ones – usually, but not always, on the same site. Nevertheless many of the top-ranking Gothic revival architects are represented, and nowadays there is much more appreciation of their work than when I was a student. Where an earlier abandoned church still exists, even as a ruin, on a different site (for example Botley and Stockbridge) I have tried to include both.

Winchester Cathedral is omitted, but that of Portsmouth and Romsey Abbey, which serve their parishes, qualify and so does Pamber Priory. Roman Catholic churches are not included, though some (post-1800) are of considerable architectural merit. It was tempting to include a few non-parochial churches of particular interest, such as the chapel of Haslar Hospital.

County boundaries have changed within the memory of some of us, particularly in the south-west of the county, where Christchurch and Bournemouth have been lost to Dorset.

The dates against the drawings relate to the year and month when they were produced, but include quite a number which I photographed then but did not use as a basis for pen-and-ink until recently. Those familiar with the churches as they are now will probably spot changes that have taken place meanwhile – less in the stones, bricks and mortar than in their surroundings. There are instances, such as Winnall, where subsequent demolition has left little trace.

My captions are only intended to give basic information, and by far the best full accounts are in the Hampshire volumes of the *Buildings of England* series published by the Pevsner Books Trust. Another useful guide has been the book by Margaret Green, simply entitled *Hampshire Churches* and published by Winton Publications Ltd in 1967. As a general rule, buildings described as Saxon can be regarded as pre-Conquest, and Norman or Romanesque as late 11th to late 12th century. The term 'Transitional' usually refers only to the merge between Norman and Early English, i.e. the start of the Gothic or pointed-arch styles. The so-called Gothic period lasted until the gradual change to classical forms in the 16th-century. The terms 'Early English', 'Decorated' and 'Perpendicular' (referring to window tracery patterns) are often used, but for simplicity I have stuck to '13th, 14th and

15th centuries' respectively, although the changes began to occur well before the ends of preceding centuries. The term 'Gothick' has come to be used for the imitation style sometimes used ornamentally around the end of the 18th century, as at Deane. The more serious copying or adaptation of medieval styles seems for no apparent reason to have tended to follow the same Norman to Perpendicular sequence in the course of the 19th century, finishing with stately buildings such as St Mary's Portsea.

The six-figure code alongside the date refers to the Ordnance Survey grid and the location map at the front of the book. Almost the whole of Hampshire falls within the O.S. square SU. Only a few places are 'SZ' and are so noted in addition to the figures. The first three figures represent 'eastings' on the grid (refer to top and bottom margins of the map) and the second three to 'northings', as explained on the margins of maps. The grid lines are 10 kilometres (6.214 miles) apart.

I am greatly indebted to my wife Elizabeth and our children Susannah and Nicholas for initiating the idea of this book, encouraging me to develop it, and helping in many ways towards its fruition – not least when I could no longer drive – or cycle – in order to refresh my memory and fill in gaps. I'm more than grateful to Andrew Illes of Phillimore Book Publishing, whose expertise has ensured the putting of it all into publishable form, and to Nigel Atkinson, Lord-Lieutenant of the county, for generously giving it his blessing with a kind foreword.

FOREWORD BY NIGEL ATKINSON
HER MAJESTY'S LORD-LIEUTENANT OF HAMPSHIRE

This fine book *An Anthology of Hampshire Churches* by Anthony New will I hope encourage Hampshire residents to visit older churches across the county and explore their architecture and contents.

The National Churches Trust have just published some recent statistics about visiting churches and made the point that many counties excel in particular features. For example, if you are specially interested in church monuments, with their sculpture, costumes and family associations, you should go to Northamptonshire. If churchyards particularly appeal then Shropshire is your choice, for spacious interiors, Norfolk, or historic 'atmosphere', Cumbria.

I venture to suggest that the county of Hampshire contains such a variety of town and village churches that it is quite unnecessary to go beyond its boundaries to find churches of surpassing interest, in any of those categories. Think, for instance, of Chawton, the church, village and great house with their memories of Jane Austen. Think of the lavish monument at Titchfield to the Earls of Southampton. Think of the tiny Saxon church of Boarhunt, of the unspoilt Georgian interior of Avington, or of the multi-coloured Itchen Stoke in a totally different Victorian style. Think of Nursling, the little backwater almost swallowed up by Southampton, whence St Boniface set out to convert the Germans to Christianity.

You may ask what might distinguish our churches from those of other counties. It is the extensive use of timber, which was always available from the once much more extensive forests, coupled with the equally ready supply of flints. Stone is relatively scarce and usually has to come from outside, while bricks were not much made and used before Georgian times. Many of the Victorian architects followed traditional timber practice, and I notice many examples of wooden bell-turrets amongst Mr New's drawings, as well as examples of what we call 'half-timber' work. But where adequate funds were available (as was sometimes the case from wealthy estates), London-based architects were not slow in specifying first-rate stone for such grand buildings as St Mary's at Privett and St Mary's, Andover – both on the sites of relatively humble predecessors.

I congratulate the author on his lifetime's work of compilation and research about our churches and their history and wish the book every success.

NIGEL ATKINSON

⋏ ABBOTTS ANN 331435

St Mary

October 1960

To the south-west of Andover. Brick and stone, 1715-16, probably by John James. Victorian tracery in some windows. Delightfully unspoiled 18th-century interior with gallery and box pews. Royal arms of 1718. Maiden garlands of hazelwood, tributes carried in funeral processions of local unmarried ladies – relics of a custom long forgotten elsewhere.

⋎ ALDERSHOT 869499

St Michael

July 1998

On Church Hill, south-east of the railway station. Mostly 1910-11 by Sir Thomas Jackson, skilfully incorporating on its south side the old village church, i.e. the 15th-century chancel (now a side chapel), brick nave of 1865, and sturdy 16th-century brick and ironstone tower. Parish hall on north side, 1997.

⋎ ALTON 718397

St Laurence

July 1946

In the town. Norman tower, early 12th-century, originally central, enhanced by its 19th-century spire. Animal carvings on capitals of tower arches, a rare feature at so early a date. Nave and chancel rebuilt against its north side in 15th century. All Perpendicular externally. Fine 17th-century pulpit. Some 15th- and 16th-century brasses.

⋎ ALVERSTOKE SZ 602988

St Mary

September 2003

The mother church of Gosport, amongst its western suburbs and seen here across a neighbouring garden. Chancel rebuilt 1865 and nave 1885 by Henry Woodyer in a rather ornate Decorated style. Tower 1904-05 by another architect. Spacious interior with many 18th-century memorials.

▼ ANDOVER 366458

St Mary

April 1995

Totally rebuilt on its commanding town site 1840-46, an early example of Early English revival, by the little-known Augustus Livesay and, later, Sydney Smirke. Plaster-vaulted interior praised by Pevsner as 'sensational', the double-traceried apse with tall screen on iron shafts being 'the climax of this ingenious and fervent design'. Stained glass of assorted dates. Some 17th- and 18th-century monuments. Twelfth-century doorway re-erected as entrance from the street.

▲ AMPORT 299443

St Mary

May 1999

Four miles west of Andover. Cruciform in plan with central tower and (unusually for Hampshire) Decorated in style. Rescued from ruin 1866-67 by Slater and Carpenter and thus largely of that date. Fifteenth-century alabaster panel with saints and angels. A wealth of 19th-century stained glass including work by James Powell and Henry Holiday.

∀ APPLESHAW 303491

St Peter

August 1994

North-west of Andover, on the Wiltshire border. Rebuilt 1839-31 by T.M. Shurmur to cruciform plan. Plaster tunnel vaults throughout. Curious little font on a column in north transept.

⋏ ASHE 534500

Holy Trinity and St Andrew

May 2018

Between Whitchurch and Basingstoke, hidden down a leafy lane near the source of the Test. Rebuilt 1877-8 by George Gilbert Scott the younger, re-using the east window stonework. Notable series of windows by Kempe and Co.

⅄ ASHLEY 386309

St Mary

August 1993

South-east of Stockbridge. In the care of Churches Conservation Trust. Norman, within a disappeared hilltop castle. Interior mostly 19th-century, with two older monuments and traces of 13th-century wall-painting.

⅄ ASHMANSWORTH 411566

St James

September 1999

On high ground near the Andover to Newbury road. Norman, except east wall. Eighteenth-century pulpit and faded 13th-century wall-paintings. The composer Gerald Finzi (d.1956) is remembered with engraved glass by Laurence Whistler in the brick porch of 1694, and with a slate headstone lettered by Reynolds Stone.

⋏ AVINGTON 533323

St Mary

July 1975

On the Itchen, between Winchester and Alresford. Rebuilt in brick 1768-71, its designer unknown. Outstanding galleried interior of the period, as complete and perfect as any in the whole country – mahogany box-pews, 'three-decker' pulpit with tester, marble font, reredos, chandelier. Monuments include one to the foundress Duchess of Chandos.

⋎ BARTON STACEY 435412

All Saints

April 1963

Five miles south-east of Andover. Internally mostly 13th-century, but outside much renewed. Curious arrangement of chancel arch springing from arcade piers, with side arches over aisles. Tower early 16th-century. Square 12th-century font. Seventeenth-century Flemish figures in altar table, with patterned medieval floor tiles around.

⌄ BASING 666529

St Mary

June 1949

At Old Basing, on the Loddon just east of Basingstoke. Norman central tower with mid-16th-century brick upper part. Remainder part flint, part brick, mostly of about 1430 onwards, but the side chapels were added in the 16th century by the Paulet family, whose arched monuments are formally disposed in pairs on either side of chancel. Their heraldry and other details are of more than usual interest. Early 16th-century statue of Virgin and Child re-set on west front.

➢ BASINGSTOKE 635522

St Michael

August 1943

Spacious clerestoried 15th-century town church with traces of its Norman predecessor. Repaired after bomb damage in the Second World War. South chapel 14th-century. Two-storied south porch c.1540. War memorial north chapel by Sir Charles Nicholson, 1920, with Flemish triptych of 1549. No fewer than four Royal arms, from Elizabeth I to Elizabeth II.

The Holy Ghost Chapel is an evocative medieval ruin within the cemetery on Chapel Hill (634526). Parts of a west tower, and of attached brick and stone Guild Chapel. Not to be confused with Holy Ghost R.C. Church nearby.

∀ BAUGHURST   582600

St Stephen

November 2003

Five miles north-west of Basingstoke. Rebuilt 1845-6 by Benjamin Ferrey, preserving the early 13th-century west doorway and 15th-century font. Some 16th-century woodwork in chancel screen.

BEAULIEU   388026

Blessed Virgin and Child

May 1962

Up the Beaulieu river from the Solent. The 13th-century refectory (dining hall) of the Cistercian abbey, preserved as a church whilst the rest fell to ruin. That explains the orientation, with altar at north end. Huge buttress at south end. Graceful arcaded stair within side wall leading to the projecting pulpit.

⌄ BEDHAMPTON 703070

St Thomas à Becket

May 1966

Just west of Havant. Chancel arch 12th-century Nave and chancel 13th- and 14th-century respectively but much renewed. North aisle and bellcote 1878.

⌃ BENTLEY 784447

St Mary

May 2001

Between Alton and Haslemere. Basically 12th-century but with many 13th-century and later changes. Clerestoried chancel. Brick tower top 18th-century. Square 12th-century font. Some early 15th-century glass, and much of 19th-century by Hardman & Co.

⌄ BENTWORTH 665403

St Mary

May 1998

West of Alton. Mostly of c.1200. Bold arcades with scalloped capitals. Tower arch, belfry and tower top by Aston Webb 1890-91. Thirteenth-century dog-tooth ornament in east window surround and in piscina.

⌃ BIGHTON 610345

All Saints

July 1995

Close to the north-east of Alresford, Chancel early 12th-century. Nave arcades slightly later. Porch and vestry of 1836, when also the weatherboarded tower was reconstructed. Delicate chancel screen and painted waggon roof panelling by Ninian Comper, c.1900. Later pulpit by his son Sebastian.

❯ BINSTED   772410

Holy Cross

November 2001

Between Alton and Farnham. A fine large
church, mostly late 12th-century and
thus Early English in character, including
tower, and nave clerestory. Chancel
arch heightened in 19th century, but the
unusual east-facing windows above are
13th-century. Big north transept added in
14th century. Rare feature of angelus bellcote on east face of tower. Also unusual
for Hampshire is the 18th-century spire
behind a parapet.

⌁ BISHOPSTOKE   467198

St Mary

August 1993

Between Winchester and Southampton. Rebuilt 1890-91 on new site by
E.P. Warren, architect also of the main building of Bedales School at Steep. By
Bainbridge Reynolds an interpretation in ironwork of the form of a medieval
chancel screen and rood. Pulpit from the previous church (of which some stones
still stand by the Itchen).

11

⌄ BISHOPS SUTTON 605320

St Nicholas

July 1946

Just east of Alresford. Norman nave.
Timber framework inside, supporting
bell turret. Chancel late 13th-century,
Piscina on north side showing that
there was once a north chapel.

The churches on this page were
amongst the many churches I visited by
bicycle from H.M.S. *Mercury* (Leydene)
on summer evenings, often several at a
time, whenever the weather was kind and
it was permissible to 'go ashore'. Often
I would clock up 25 miles or so before
daylight faded. Consequently those pencil
sketches were done far too hastily!

⌃ BISHOPS WALTHAM 556176

St Peter

July 1946

Wide nave probably also Norman in origin. Arcades c.1200 but reconstructed.
Aisles 17th-century, curiously late for Gothic. Tower at south-west, 16th-century.
Pulpit of 1626, quite a showpiece. Some interesting 18th-century monuments in the
church and headstones in the churchyard.

⅄ BLENDWORTH 711135

Holy Trinity

January 2018

Between Petersfield and Havant. Rebuilt on new site by W.G. and E. Habershon in a Victorian variant of Decorated, replacing the demolished St Giles'. Memorable for a winter visit by car, with my wife driving. Another call was needed to retrieve my umbrella, which a kind parishioner had found and placed in the church – one of the hazards of out-of-season exploration!

⋏ BOARHUNT 603083

St Nicholas

July 1946

Charmingly rural, in spite of nearness to Portsmouth, a few miles to its south-east. Expertly dated to the 1060s. Plain chancel arch indeed of that period, but windows slightly enlarged later. Big rough font probably Saxon. Equally unfussy pitch pine woodwork 19th-century.

◄ BOLDRE 323993

St John

June 1959

Picturesquely on its own at the edge of the New Forest, just north of Lymington. South arcade late 12th-century, the north a little later, and the western extension of the south aisle later still. Tower c.1300 at the base, but belfry 1697, of brick. Memorial tablet of 1804 to rector William Gilpin, an early writer on landscape for travellers.

◄ BOSSINGTON 337309

St James

April 2000

In a tiny place on the Test three miles south of Stockbridge, a little 'estate' church rebuilt 1839-40. Glass in three windows by the Whall family. Early 17th-century pulpit.

⋎ BOTLEY 510120

St Bartholomew

June 2018

Six miles east of Southampton. All that survives of the little old church of St Bartholomew, adjoining Manor Farm Country Park and well to the south of the present town. The west end having been demolished by a falling tree, the eastern part is closed off by a wall with reassembled bits of a 12th-century doorway. Simple furnishings, a few memorials and the old parish bier, a precious relic. All Saints' superseded it in 1836.

⋏ All Saints 512130

June 2018

Of this the chancel was rebuilt in 1859. North aisle added and nave re-roofed with dormers 1893-95 by Sir Thomas Jackson. Foyer and ancillary rooms added at west end 2006, with careful alignment of roof levels and repetition of dormers. From the old church the 12th-century font, unusually on a hexagonal stem and base, and a fine 14th-century canopied tomb.

ⴸ BRAMDEAN 609277

SS Simon and Jude

February 2008

Between Petersfield and Winchester. Basically Norman, with various alterations and additions. Chancel arch later 12th-century, just pointed and thus very early Gothic. Brick north porch 1733. Large south transept 19th-century.

ⴸ BRADLEY 636418

All Saints

May 1998

West of Alton, off the Basingstoke road. Early 13th-century, quite small and largely rebuilt 1875-7. Low 14th-century arcade. Quaint 'home-made' pulpit of 1921, framed with little tree trunks at the angles.

⛢ BRAMLEY 644590

St James

August 2002

A few miles north of Basingstoke. Late 12th-century without aisles, dominated outside by south transeptal brick Brocas Chapel of 1801-03 by Sir John Soane (but the big window is of 1889). Highly interesting interior including 13th-century wall-paintings, gallery of 1728, 15th-century screen, 16th-century bench-ends, and in the plaster-vaulted chapel a giant marble monument to Bernard Brocas, 1777, as well as 16th-century Flemish glazing.

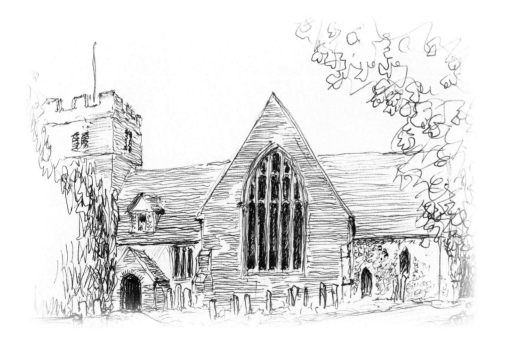

⛢ BRAMSHAW 265166

St Peter

October 2000

Close to the Wiltshire border, south of the Salisbury to Southampton road. South tower prominently against a road, with two bells, one 13th-century. Nave 13th-century too. Remainder of brick, rebuilt to cruciform plan by John Peniston, 1829.

BRAMSHOTT 843328

St Mary

October 1956

Close to the Surrey and Sussex borders. Cruciform with additions. Chancel Early English but tower, spire and transepts c.1400. Nave and aisles 1871-72 by Sylvester Capes – who also changed the west and east arches of the tower. Earthenware jars found in tower walls, probably an acoustic device. East window glass in memory of Canadian troops who trained on the Common.

BREAMORE 153189

St Mary

January 2003

North of Fordingbridge on the Salisbury road. Also cruciform, an important Saxon survival, of about the millennium, A.D. 1000. Of that date the whole south transept with its arch, also west ends of chancel walls, typical 'long-and-short' walling in nave, and two nave windows. North transept truncated. South doorway 12th-century and other parts 14th-century, but over the doorway a monumental but sadly damaged 11th-century Crucifixion.

⋎ BROUGHTON 309329

St Mary

September 1996

South-west of Stockbridge. Mostly Early English including arcades (the north with scalloped capitals). Tower 15th-century with belfry stage of 1845. Fifteenth-century piscina with carving of devil catching man in noose. Sixteenth-century Dutch painting of Lamentation in small central panel of reredos. Round brick dovecote in churchyard 1684, with revolving central ladder.

⋏ BROCKENHURST 305017

St Peter

June 1959

Between Lyndhurst and Lymington. Twelfth-century nave. Thirteenth-century chancel. Brick tower 1761. North aisle 1832 with iron columns. Giant yew tree.

⌄ BROWN CANDOVER   581396

St Peter

August 1943

A few miles north of Alresford. Rebuilt 1845 by T.H. Wyatt. Flint and stone. Seventeenth-century communion rail from old church of Northington, thought to be Flemish. Brass of c.1500 depicting couple with interlinked arms.

⌃ BULLINGTON   455413

St Michael

April 1963

Between Winchester and Whitchurch, near the A34 and A303 junction. Nave 12th-century and chancel 13th-century, but much rebuilt by Ewan Christian 1871.

❯ BURGHCLERE 468579

All Saints

September 1998

At Old Burghclere six miles south of Newbury, and not to be confused with the 19th-century church of the Ascension in Burghclere village. Nave with Norman doorways north and south. Chancel and north transept 13th-century. Bell-turret 19th-century. Much 19th-century furnishing, but pews c.1600, good and substantial.

⌂ BURITON 740200

St Mary

July 1946

Close to the south of Petersfield. Stone tower of 1714, retaining unusually massive 13th-century arch to nave. Nave arcades late 12th-century with scalloped capitals. Wide roof right across nave and aisles, a so-called 'catslide'. Chancel late 13th-century with exceptionally fine triple sedilia and fragmentary wall-paintings.

⚓ BURSLEDON 488097

St Leonard

September 1962

Between Southampton and Fareham. Largely of 1888 by J.P. Sedding, including transepts and whole west end with much ornamental woodwork. Thirteenth-century walling in chancel and its arch. Norman font. Tablets to local craftsmen, one of 1691 with representations of brickmaking tools and one of 1794 with relief of ship.

⌄ CATHERINGTON 696145

All Saints

November 2006

Near A3, south-west of Petersfield. Mostly late 12th-century, enjoying a fine view southwards. Externally much renewed 1883. Good 14th-century woodwork in nave roof. Painting of same period on north wall, St Michael weighing souls. North chapel dominated by canopied tomb of Sir Nicholas Hyde, d.1631.

⅄ CHARLTON 351471

St Thomas

June 2018

In a north-west suburb of Andover, memorable for a very hot day when the local inn was seething with football fans hoping to watch television! Small church built 1908 by H.C. Benson, replacing the demolished one at Foxcott, from which a 15th-century niche was transferred.

⋀ CHALTON 732159

St Michael

June 1946

Amongst the Downs between Petersfield and Havant. Impressive Early English chancel with fine 'Geometric' tracery in east window. Nave and south transept perhaps c.1300 or earlier. Tower much less imposing, with 18th-century brick battlements.

❯ CHAWTON 708370

St Nicholas

Close to the south-west of Alton, and to Chawton House, home of the Austen family. Rebuilt 1871-2 by Sir Arthur Blomfield, with fragments only of medieval walling in chancel. Communion rail 18th-century. Some good 19th-century stained glass. Central Crucifixion painting in reredos attributed to Frans Francken, c.1600. Standing monument to Sir Richard Knight, died 1679. Others to his later family. Nineteenth-century tablets to Jane Austen's mother Cassandra and sister Cassandra Elizabeth.

▲ CHERITON 582285

St Michael

July 1946

South of Alresford on the little Itchen, perched on a prehistoric long barrow within the scattered village. Tower late 12th-century. Remainder mostly Early English with some Perpendicular windows. Patches of brickwork amongst the flint result from repair after a fire in 1744. Unexplained 14th-century traceried triangles and carved heads on either side of south porch.

⋎ CHILBOLTON 394403

St Mary

July 1995

In the Test valley south-east of Andover. Long 13th-century chancel. Aisles added in 14th century, leaving some evidence of a former early Norman nave in a little window high above the south arcade. Tower 1842. Good late 16th-century pulpit.

⋎ CHILCOMB 507279

St Andrew

December 1991

Near the east side of Winchester, blissfully hidden from nearby main roads. Early Norman with a tiny chancel arch. Curious octagonal font set on a medieval stone coffin lid, possibly 18th-century.

⌄ CHILTON CANDOVER 592403

St Nicholas

August 2003

A few miles north of Alresford. The church collapsed and was demolished in 1878. Its 12th-century crypt, a rectangular tunnel-vaulted chamber ending in a small apse, was re-discovered in 1927 and made accessible. Several medieval tomb slabs and a 12th-century font.

⌃ CHILWORTH 407188

St Denys

August 1993

Close to Southampton on its north side. Rebuilt 1812-20 in stuccoed brick. Typical of the period, so-called Gothick, with attractively plaster-vaulted interior. Gothic panels on pew-ends, and Gothic patterns in the wrought-iron communion rail. From the earlier building not only a 12th-century font but also two 12th-century bells, said to be the oldest in the southern counties.

CHRISTCHURCH

Formerly in Hampshire, is now in Dorset.

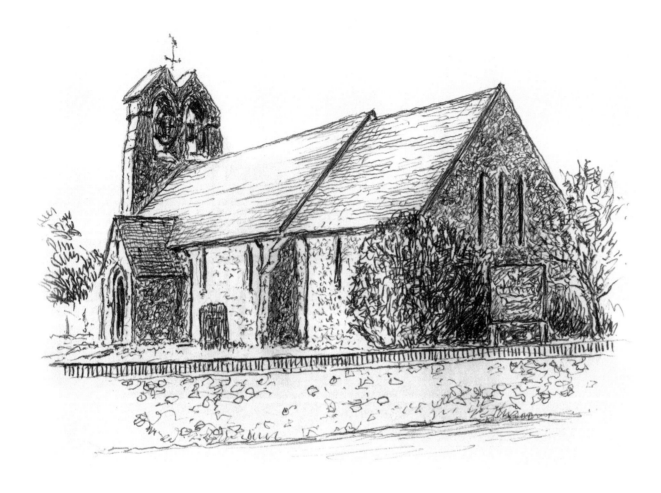

⋎ CLIDDESDEN 633491

St Leonard

August 1943

Close to Basingstoke on the south. Largely 15th-century, but north wall 12th-century, with unusually large flints in regular courses, and a 12th-century doorway. Fine 15th-century roof to nave. All extensively repaired and embellished in 19th century.

⋏ CLANFIELD 697168

St James

December 2006

Over the Downs in an expanded village south of Petersfield. Rebuilt 1875. Flint and stone outside and patterned brick interior. Big bellcote and re-used 15th-century west window. Fourteenth-century font.

27

⋎ COLEMORE 706308

St Peter ad Vincula

November 2001

On a quiet lane six miles south of Alton. Twelfth-century cruciform, but missing its south transept. Bell-turret 1975, i.e. renewed since the Churches Conservation Trust took the church over. North transept the least altered part, with unusual doorway in its west wall. Font Norman too, Purbeck 'marble'.

COMBE

Formerly in Hampshire, is now in Berkshire.

⋏ COMPTON 467256

All Saints

August 1993

Close to M3 south of Winchester. All 12th-century, except south aisle and chapel of 1905 and bell-turret. Quite elaborate north doorway with zigzag ornament. Font 12th-century too.

⌄ CORHAMPTON   611204

No known dedication

June 1946

On the Meon valley road north-east of Bishops Waltham. Unmistakably Saxon, perhaps c.1020, with typical long-and-short stones at the quoins, and thin lesenes (pilaster strips) punctuating the walls. Chancel arch original too, but east end rebuilt in inappropriate brickwork after collapsing in 1842. Thirteenth-century wall-paintings. Saxon sundial to right of entrance, showing division of day into eight 'tides'.

⌃ CRAWLEY   424348

St Mary

August 1993

Between Winchester and Stockbridge. Nave and aisles late 14th-century, remarkable for oak arcades and roofs, their workmanship not unlike a farm barn. Chancel 13th-century (much rebuilt), tower 1901. Meeting room added at west end since the date of the sketch.

⋎ CROFTON 551042

Holy Rood

August 1998

Two miles south-west of Fareham. A little ancient church, now superseded for parish purposes by that of Stubbington with the same dedication built in 1878. Nave probably 15th-century with a fine roof, perhaps with ships' timbers re-used. South transept early 19th-century. Remainder largely 14th-century, but west wall with bellcote rebuilt in brick in 18th century. Unspoilt homely interior. Pulpit perhaps 18th-century. Some wall-tablets, including a large one to Thomas Missing, died 1733.

⋎ CRONDALL 795485

All Saints

August 2002

Between Odiham and Farnham and here viewed from the east. One of the most impressive churches of Hampshire, not least for the sturdy brick tower of 1659 which replaced a central one. Unusual external galleried connections with the older stair turret. Nave and aisles late 12th-century, thus Transitional between Norman and Early English. Giant 16th-century buttresses, especially at west end. Chancel of exquisite Early English design, stone-vaulted. Saxon font, quite plain. In the chancel floor the fine brass of a 14th-century rector. Many interesting monuments of 17th and 18th centuries.

⌄ DAMERHAM   107158

St George

August 1956

Or South Damerham, west of Fordingbridge and formerly in Wiltshire. Ambitious tower begun in 12th century with a north arch to the nave. continued perhaps in the 17th century and then petering out (to quote Pevsner) with a weatherboarded top. Whether it was meant for a transept (as it now is) is uncertain. North arcade 12th-century and south 13th-century. Chancel apparently 15th-century but with blocked arcades in north and south walls, indicating former aisle-chapels. Tympanum over 12th-century inner south doorway with carving of St George and Dragon. Prominent stump and steps of churchyard Cross.

⌃ CRUX EASTON   425563

St Michael

March 1962

On high ground near the Andover to Newbury road. Rebuilt in brick 1775. Of that period the effectively simple chancel panelling and floor, pulpit, eagle lectern, marble font, and even the wrought-iron churchyard gates (by-passed by the steps depicted).

⋁ DEANE 546503

All Saints

October 1960

Between Whitchurch and Basingstoke. In parkland. Rebuilt 1818-20 as thank-offering for victory at Waterloo. No aisles but remarkable for the extensive use of imitation Gothic details in Coade stone, artificially produced in Lambeth in that period (the recipe is lost). Pretty chancel screen, ceilings and altar surround.

⋀ DIBDEN 397087

All Saints

February 2000

On the west side of Southampton Water. Severely damaged by a bomb in 1940. Tower of 1884. Nave rebuilt by Pinckney and Gott without aisles, the north and south walls on the lines of the destroyed arcades. Chancel walls left in damaged state as a memorial, 13th- and 14th-centuries. Wall-arcading, unusual for a church of its size. Good east window of 1950s by Derek Wilson.

⅄ DOGMERSFIELD 782526

All Saints

June 2018

North-east of Odiham. Completely rebuilt 1843 by Benjamin Ferrey in Early English style, with a reredos painting Burial of Christ believed to be by Van Dyck. A small and unexceptional previous church in the village is now a house, and superseded yet another on a third site. Some older monuments have ended up in the present building.

⅄ DROXFORD 607183

St Mary and All Saints

June 1946

In the Meon valley east of Bishops Waltham. Spotted by the rector whilst doing this sketch, I was commissioned to do a better one for the parish magazine cover! Quite a complex church in its evolution. Nave 12th-century, north arcade later 12th-century, south arcade early 13th-century, chapel arcades early 14th-century, and tower of 1599 with curious diagonally set stair turret. Main roof a 'catslide' over nave and aisles but chancel 18th-century – with internal cornice which continues hidden above the nave's later plaster vault. Good 13th-century female effigy in south chapel, found buried in a field.

➤ DURLEY 505169

Holy Cross

June 1946

A chapel to Upham, but some distance from its own village north of Botley. Cruciform, probably c.1300. Pulpit and sounding board dated 1630, quite ambitious for the size of the building.

🡑 DUMMER 589460

All Saints

September 1967

Near M3 to the south-west of Basingstoke. Chancel c.1200, but nave probably earlier. Fifteenth-century nave roof with rare panelled rood canopy. Sturdy bell-turret and 17th-century gallery extending along half of nave. Communion rail of same period. Unusually early wooden pulpit, late 14th-century.

➤ EAST DEAN 274267

St Winfrith

April 2000

Close to Wiltshire, north-west of Romsey. Basically Norman, but much altered in succeeding centuries, with simple timber bell-turret and other woodwork. Eighteenth-century gallery and small font. The head of the north doorway is made from a single piece of oak, probably 17th-century.

➢ EAST MEON   681223

All Saints

May 1946

Amongst the finest churches of Hampshire, not least for the 12th-century central tower with apparently original broach spire, seen against a grassy South Downs hill by the growing upper Meon. To me it became a familiar sight when travelling to and from Leydene, and many years ago I used a similar view for a Christmas card. Nave and chancel and south transept late 11th-century. Arcades to south aisle and chapel both early 13th-century but differing in details. Equally thrilling is the 12th-century font of black Tournai marble, like the one in Winchester Cathedral: boldly carved arcading, foliage and birds, and on north and east sides scenes with Adam and Eve. Pulpit of 1706, from the destroyed London church of Holy Trinity Minories. Some furnishings by Ninian Comper, including delicate reredos in Lady (south) Chapel, 1910. Also by Comper are the First World War memorial east window and other glass, as well as the lychgate.

◄   St Nicholas' Chapel   656240

August 2007

At Westbury, 1¼ miles north-west. A picturesque ruin by the Meon, probably 13th-century. Its small 12th-century font is now in All Saints' church.

⋎ EASTON   509322

St Mary

July 1946

By the Itchen, north-east of Winchester. Late Norman, somewhat disguised by Woodyer's fancy remodelling of the west tower-top in the 1860s. Chancel and its east apse both vaulted, very unusually for a village church. Monument of 1595 to Agnes Barlow, a bishop's widow whose five daughters married five bishops.

⋎ EAST STRATTON   541401

All Saints

September 1967

In the middle of the county, close to M3. Rebuilt 1885-90 by Sir Thomas Jackson in elaborate Perpendicular style on a new site. That of the previous church (of 1810) is marked by a cross at the south end of the adjoining park.

∀ EAST TISTED   701323

St James the Great

November 2001

South of Alton on the Fareham road. Nearly all rebuilt 1846 and less correctly neo-Gothic than would be expected a decade or so later – here for example are cast-iron window frames, and classical cherubs' heads in the roof. Little is medieval except the tower base and chancel arch. The main interest is in the monuments, particularly the 16th-century arched tomb of Richard Norton with its mixture of Gothic and Renaissance detail.

∀ EAST TYTHERLEY   292290

St Peter

April 2000

Close to the Wiltshire border, well to the east of Salisbury. Basically 13th-century though much renewed, with tower of 1897. Unusually early stained glass: three little 13th-century figures in the chancel. Elizabethan monument to Gifford family, moved and re-assembled with figures looking in wrong directions.

⅋ EAST WELLOW   303204

St Margaret

August 1994

Near the Wiltshire border, west of Romsey. Associations with Florence Nightingale. Her family memorial pillar is in the churchyard, south of porch, with simple inscription 'F.N.' and dates. Chancel and nave 13th-century. Weather-boarded tower on wooden posts within nave, dormer windows, and south aisle separated by single post and beams - probably all 18th-century. Extensive series of 13th-century wall-paintings including fine St Christopher and Christ Child on north wall.

⅄ EAST WOODHAY   405615

St Martin

September 1999

Between the Downs and the county border (West Woodhay is in Berkshire). Nave rebuilt in brick 1822-23 by Richard Billing and Son. Flint-faced chancel 1850. Some window surrounds altered since. Pugin-designed window at south-west of chancel. Fine monument to Edward Goddard (died 1724) and wife Elizabeth with figures in ordinary attire – by sculptor Francis Bird.

⌄ EAST WORLDHAM   751382

St Mary

October 1956

Just east of Alton, very visible from the east. Early 13th-century, with nicely detailed window and doorway stonework. Somewhat altered 1864-66 by David Brandon, with new roof and bellcote.

⌃ ECCHINSWELL   502598

St Laurence

August 2003

In an attractive village beneath the Downs west of Kingsclere. Rebuilt 1886 by Bodley and Garner, on a new site half a mile to the north of the old. Commendably simple nave, short aisles, chancel and south chapel. Screen and rood beam instead of chancel arch. Tower with weatherboarded belfry and shingled spire. Only the 15th-century font saved from old church. Nearby Nuthanger Farm features in Richard Adams' novel *Watership Down*.

↴ ELING   367126

St Mary

February 2000

On a creek at the head of Southampton Water. Largely
medieval of various dates, but much altered inside
and renewed outside by Benjamin Ferrey 1863-65 and
consequently hard to analyse. Two Saxon windows apparently
not in situ. Fine large chancel arch. south arcade late 12th-
century, the north 13th-century, curtailed by tower added
perhaps in 16th century. Reredos painting of Last Supper,
16th-century, Venetian. Numerous wall-tablets.

↑ ELLINGHAM   44084

St Mary

May 2001

In the Avon valley, just north of Ringwood, largely 13th-
century. Brick porch of 1720 with large blue painted sundial.
Jacobean pulpit, with hourglass attached to simple 15th-
century screen. Eighteenth-century communion rail, also
reredos attributed to Grinling Gibbons, moved to west end.

▼ ELLISFIELD 639459

St Martin

May 1998

Amongst the Downs south of Basingstoke. Basically 12th-century, but very much renewed. Tower (out of the picture on the left) 1884. Seventeenth-century communion rail.

▲ ELVETHAM 783565

St Mary

October 1956

In the north-east of the county, close to Fleet. The church stands in the grounds of the Elvetham (Hall) Hotel and is deconsecrated. Rebuilt 1840-41 by Henry Roberts. Spire with curious gargoyles and Evangelists' symbols, attributed to Samuel Teulon, architect of the Hall. Twin early 18th-century monuments to Reynolds Calthorpe and wife.

⊻ EMPSHOTT 754313

Holy Rood

September 1946

Between Petersfield and Alton. A specially good small example of Early English design, with white clunch (chalk) arcades on alternate round and octagonal piers. The narrowness of the aisles is thought to result from 17th-century rebuilding of outer walls. West porch also 17th-century but bell-turret of 1884, with unusual glazed upper storey. Font 13th-century with cover of 1626. Tower screen and choir stalls 17th-century too. Pulpit with 'linenfold' panels perhaps c.1530.

◄ EVERSLEY 79610

St Mary

May 1942

Near the Berkshire and Surrey borders. This pencil sketch marked my introduction to Hampshire churches at the age of 17. I had cycled from Barnet to stay at nearby Bracknell with an aunt who had retreated there from the South London bombs. The strong brick tower dates from 1735. At about that time a new nave was added to the medieval church on the south but with the short brick south chapel of c.1500 becoming the chancel. The former nave became the north aisle and in 1875-76 was rebuilt with classical arcade and new tower arch by Bodley and Garner – as a memorial to Charles Kingsley, who was rector for three decades. New rooms on the north side date from 1996. In the chancel floor is a notable brass to Richard Pendilton, 1502. Several 17th-century and later monuments.

▼ EXBURY 427003

St Catherine

June 2000

Close to the Beaulieu river on the edge of the New Forest. Built 1907 by J. Oldrid Scott, supplanting a building of 1827, and before that an older church at Lower Exbury. From the last came the 13th-century font and a bell of 1509. First World War soldier's bronze effigy, a memorial to two sons of Lord Forster.

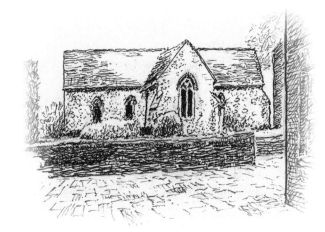

▲ EWHURST 570567

No dedication

November 2004

In the north of the county, with no village. Hemmed in by the big house and stables and rebuilt 1873. Now used as a store. Fifteenth-century east window. Monument of 1789 to the then estate owner.

⋎ EXTON 614211

SS Peter and Paul

July 1946

In the Meon valley. Largely 13th-century but much renewed. Striking 'Arts and Crafts' east window glass and painted surround by Charles Spooner, 1900 – 'Tree of Life'. Headstone brought in from churchyard carved with old man ('Father Time'?) in his library: the name and date are lost.

⋎ FACCOMBE 390581

St Barnabas

September 1999

The parish church of Netherton close to Berkshire and Wiltshire, rebuilt on a fresh site one mile further west in 1865-66 by G.B. Musselwhite. His chancel was taken down in 1965. From the old church were brought the Norman font and a few monuments.

➤ FAREHAM 575062

SS Peter and Paul

July 1946

A town church that has seen major changes. The sturdy brick tower with cupola was built in 1742 against the north side of the original stone nave. A bigger nave with aisles was built in 1812, so the old chancel arch (c.1200) leads into what became a north chapel. In 1888 the chancel was rebuilt in a Gothic style by Sir Arthur Blomfield. His intended nave was never built, but in 1930-31 Sir Charles Nicholson swept away most of the 1812 work and replaced it with a new brick-faced nave and aisles, a precursor of his 1938-39 enlargement of Portsmouth Cathedral but Gothic-arched. Against the tower he added an outer aisle with brick porch. The old north chapel is a 'museum' area with panels of a 15th-century screen, some of the numerous memorial tablets, and at its north-east angle some Saxon 'long-and-short' work.

▽ FARLEIGH WALLOP 625475

St Andrew

May 1998

Not far to the south of Basingstoke, nowhere near the other Wallops. Rebuilt in the 1730s to a cruciform plan, flint-faced with brick quoins, and much altered to a late Gothic style in 1871-72. Tower added 1873. Eighteenth-century altar rail, with addition of heraldic goats which came from the demolished Hurstbourne Park. Interesting series of memorials to the Wallop family, including a tablet using a beautifully carved wood garland as a frame.

❧ FARLEY CHAMBERLAYNE 397275

St John

August 1993

Far from towns and truly rural, in itself and in its surroundings – except that the boundary wall has latterly been insensitively rebuilt. The south doorway flanked by odd faces confirms the church's Norman origin. But the big windows and dormer are 18th-century and the roofs and bell-turret probably earlier. Pulpit and canopy, communion rail and baluster font 18th-century. Monuments to St John family.

⛰ FARLINGTON 68605

St Andrew

September 2018

On the old coastal road, west of Havant. Rebuilt in 1872-75 by George Edmund Street and regarded as one of his best small churches. Vaulted chancel using two stone colours, enhanced by the colours of stained glass also mostly designed by him. Some medieval stonework retained at west end.

⛰ FARNBOROUGH 873556

St Peter

October 1956

In Church Avenue, a short way south-east of the railway station. Much of the nave Norman, including north and south doorways, the latter protected by a fine 16th-century timber porch. Wooden also the west tower, perhaps late 17th-century. Chancel rebuilt bigger in 1886, augmented by transepts in 1963-64. South aisle of 1900-01 by Sir Arthur Blomfield. Chancel screen and west gallery early 17th-century. Wall-paintings of female saints on north wall including St Eugenia (the proximity to Empress Eugenie's mausoleum at the nearby Abbey is apparently fortuitous), probably c.1200.

⌄ FARRINGDON 713355

All Saints

July 1946

Close to the south of Alton. Robust Norman north arcade with extraordinarily wide arches. Chancel rebuilt 1858 by the long-serving rector T.H. Massey who also built the nearby giant red brick many-roomed 'Folly'. South porch 17th- and 18th-centuries. Curious composite font of three different periods with scrolled Jacobean cover. Many 13th-century patterned tiles in chancel floor.

⋎ FAWLEY 457035

All Saints

January 1980

Close to the east of the oil refinery on Southampton Water so, not surprisingly, damaged by bombing. Three-aisled, with tower unusually in middle of south side, between aisle and chapel. Basically late 12th-century, including reconstructed north chancel arcade. But other arcades 14th-century. Under the chancel east window a probably Saxon window surround, found after the bombing, has been re-set. Good Jacobean pulpit. Interesting headstones in churchyard.

⋎ FORDINGBRIDGE 145138

St Mary

May 2001

On the Avon between Ringwood and Salisbury. Mostly 13th-century, with 15th- to 16th-century alterations – including nave clerestory and big west window, two-storied north porch, upper parts of tower (on north side of church) and on the north chapel a splendid hammer-beam roof with angels, of a type found in East Anglia, rather than Hampshire. Attractively framed brass to William Bulkeley, died 1568.

∀ FREEFOLK 487486

St Nicholas

August 2003

Just east of Whitchurch in the upper Test valley. With the Churches Conservation Trust, a single cell without chancel arch, hardly changed since 1703 and with furnishings to match. Walls and roof 13th-century but stonework of small windows probably 15th-century. Screen now at west end 15th-century too. Two rather naïve 17th-century monuments.

∀ FROXFIELD 703255

St Peter

February 2008

On the plateau west of Petersfield. Rebuilt by Sir Arthur Blomfield 1887 on the site of that demolished 25 years earlier. Some interesting memorials including a headstone with two cherubim blowing the Last Trump.

⚔ FROYLE 56428

Assumption of St Mary

March 2002

Between Alton and Farnham. Generous 13th-century chancel. Brick tower 1722. Nave in between rebuilt 1812, also in brick, with porch of 1993. Brass chandelier of 1716, called 'a gorgeous piece' by Pevsner. Unusually good glass in the chancel, particularly the 14th-century heraldry in the east window tracery (the Jesse Tree below is of 1896) and 13th-century grisaille patterns in the north and south.

⚔ FYFIELD 295464

St Nicholas

August 1994

West of Andover, off the Amesbury road. Virtually rebuilt 1846-47 by Owen Carter. Only the chancel east and south window stonework is older.

⚔ GOODWORTH CLATFORD 366425

St Peter

August 1996

South of Andover in the Anton valley. A church of gradual development, once cruciform. So the two west bays of the south arcade are late 11th-century but the fourth is a little older and led to a transept. The third arch is 13th-century, with dog-tooth ornament. On the north is a matching transept arch, but only two (14th-century) to balance the south side's three. Tower 14th-century too. Aisle walls and most of the roofs 15th-century. Meeting-room of 1992-93 added on north side.

GOSPORT 621994

Holy Trinity

September 1973

Originally a chapel to Alverstoke, built in 1696, with 'arcades' of oak Ionic columns, heavy entablatures, a barrel ceiling, and east apse with panelled half-dome added in 1734. All of that still exists but disguised by Sir Arthur Blomfield's 1887 re-modelling of the brick outer walls to look rather like an Italianate basilica, complete with detached campanile. Reredos painting of Nativity believed to be 18th-century Florentine. The organ, brought in the 18th century from Canons Park in Middlesex where it was played by Handel, retains much of its original case.

St Luke 617987

June 2004

Formerly the Royal Naval Hospital Chapel and now cared for by the Haslar Heritage Trust, the red brick hospital buildings and very extensive grounds having been adapted for domestic use. Not a parish church, but to me of sentimental interest because I was given a new hip joint in the hospital in the interim period before its closure, when many of the personnel were still uniformed. The centrally placed free-standing chapel was built in 1756 by T. Jacobsen. Simple classical interior somewhat altered 1963. Gallery reduced to west end only.

GREATHAM   773304

St John Baptist

June 1946

North of Petersfield, on the Farnham road, my last stop in 1946 when I brought my bicycle from Barnet to Leydene. The old church, opposite its Victorian successor. Chancel (possibly 11th-century but with 18th-century arch) still roofed, with alabaster tomb of Dame Margery Caryll, 1632, brought in from ruined nave.

GRATELEY   275420

St Leonard

May 1999

South-west of Andover, towards the Wiltshire border. Largely 12th- and 13th-centuries, but much renewed. Medieval floor tiles in chancel. Some 13th-century glass, notably a panel in a south window depicting the Stoning of St Stephen brought from Salisbury Cathedral.

➤   St John Baptist   774303

July 2018

The 'new' church of 1875 by Liverpool architects H. and A.P. Fry. Tower and spire added 1897. All the stained glass is by Clayton and Bell. Imposing lychgate by Harry Hems of Exeter, 1907.

⌄ HALE 178186

St Mary

February 2001

On the Avon between Fordingbridge and Salisbury, in the home village of Thomas Archer, architect of Birmingham Cathedral and St John Smith Square, Westminster. A most unusual little building, with early 17th-century nave and chancel. Transepts added in 1717 by Archer, as well as a new west front, modillioned cornices on the older walls, and unorthodox classical details – not improved by some 19th-century alterations. Three exceptionally good 18th-century monuments including one to Archer himself (died 1743).

⋏ GREYWELL 718510

St Mary

October 1956

East of Basingstoke and south of Hook. Nave with tower and chancel arches c.1200. Projection on south side for later rood loft stair, now blocked though the screen remains (c.1500). Chancel rebuilt 1851 by Ewan Christian. Tower 17th-century, buttressed later.

⌄ HAMBLE 481067

St Andrew

August 2001

On the east side of Southampton Water. The church of a priory founded in 1128, and still mostly of that period, with a fine north doorway. Only the chancel was monastic, and that was altered in the 13th century. Fine east window with 'Geometric' tracery, and double piscina. Among many wall memorials is one to the pioneer pilot Sir Edwin Alliott Verdon Roe (died 1958). The sketch includes the outer screen wall of the parish hall and 'cloister' added on the south side c.1980.

⌃ HAMBLEDON 646152

SS Peter and Paul

June 1946

North of Portsmouth and south-east of Petersfield. Quite large, and too complex in its history to describe fully here. Enlarged early in the 13th century by extending the nave to occupy what was the chancel and building a new chancel beyond. So the arch half-way along the nave was the old chancel arch, and the two-bay arcades west of it are late 12th-century The three bays to the east are rather later, and all have traces of Saxon work above the arches. No aisles to 13th-century chancel. Roofs mainly medieval. Tower largely rebuilt on old base 1794, with 15th-century two-storey vestry against it. Fifteenth-century south porch, also originally with upper floor.

HANNINGTON   538544

All SS

June 1949

On high ground south of Kingsclere. The strange two-stage spire marks Benjamin Ferrey's 1858 west addition to the nave, which has Saxon work, mainly visible in the 'long-and-short' north-east quoin. The rest basically c.1200, but arcade arches and chancel arch a century later, and chancel windows later still. Engraved glass of 1988-89 by Laurence Whistler in two chancel windows, that on the south side especially beautiful.

HARBRIDGE   105142

All Saints

May 2001

Between Fordingbridge and Ringwood. Only the tower is ancient, mostly 15th-century. The rest was rebuilt in 1838 by G. Evans. Some interesting roundels of 17th-century Dutch glass.

55

HARTLEY MAUDITT 743361

St Leonard

November 2000

Between Alton and Selborne, by a large pond, the church is the survivor of a disappeared village. Twelfth-century nave, with a richly ornamented pointed-arched south doorway of c.1190 and bell-turret of 1904. Some medieval floor tiles, unusually including some with fish designs. Chancel 13th-century with colourful monuments to Steward family. That to Sir Nicholas (d. 1710) depicts a Crusader ancestor slaying a lion with a club.

HARTLEY WESPALL 698583

St Mary

October 1998

North-east of Basingstoke, near the Reading road. West wall of extraordinary design, its exposed timbers dated to about 1330. Pattern of upper members followed in waggon roof of nave. Flint walls much renewed, but with wood-framed doorways probably 15th-century. West tower removed, but that of 1868-70 on north side incorporates the frame of its belfry stage. Chancel all 19th-century. Pulpit early 17th-century. Marble monument to Lady Stawell, 1692.

⚑ HARTLEY WINTNEY 767559

St Mary

March 1957

In open country between the village and M3. Superseded by the 1870 church of St John the Evangelist and now in care of Churches Conservation Trust,. Chancel 11th- or early 12th-century. Nave 13th- or 14th-century. Brick transepts added 1834 and flint tower 1845. Interior little altered since then, with galleries, brick floors, box pews and hatchments. Seventeenth-century communion table and 18th-century rail.

⚑ HAVANT 17063

St Faith

October 1946

In the town centre. Less complex than it appears outside, but remarkable for having aisles to the transepts as well as a vaulted chancel. Nave and aisles all rebuilt 1874-5 – also central tower and its 12th-century arches with, it is said, re-used stonework. The main entrance leads confusingly into the west aisle of the north transept. Its arcade is 15th-century and that on the south a copy of it. Some interesting 18th-century wall-tablets.

⋎ HEADBOURNE WORTHY 487320

St Swithun

August 1943

Close to the north-east of Winchester. Largely early 11th-century and archaeologically of great importance for the great carved rood, flanked by the Virgin and St John. over the west doorway. All have been defaced except the Hand of God high above, but are protected by a 16th-century west annexe. Chancel extended and nave south wall rebuilt in 13th century. Tower also added then, but its timber upper part is 18th-century.

⋏ HAWKLEY 746292

SS Peter and Paul

November 2001

Four miles north of Petersfield. Rebuilt 1864-65 by Samuel Teulon in his idiosyncratic version of Romanesque. Tower with so-called 'Rhenish helm', a four-gabled steeple, modelled on that of Sompting in Sussex. High arcades on round piers, and much robust naturalistic carving. Thirteenth-century piscina from previous church, also genuinely late Norman font.

⅄ HEADLEY 518627

All Saints

October 1956

On the Wey, south of Farnham. Late 14th-century, but much renewed and chancel added 1857-59 following a fire. Nave roof nevertheless notable. A fine 13th-century stained glass panel now in north window of chancel.

⅄ HECKFIELD 723605

St Michael

October 1998

North-east of Basingstoke on the Berkshire border. Fifteenth- and early 16th-centuries, but extensively renewed, rebuilt and refurnished by William Butterfield 1876-77. Fourteenth-century Purbeck marble font. Beautiful Edward Burne-Jones window at east end of nave. Interesting memorials including 16th-century brasses and a tablet to Neville Chamberlain, d.1940.

⌄ HERRIARD 664460

St Mary

May 1998

Between Alton and Basingstoke. Early 13th-century, but tower and north aisle by John Colson, 1876-77. Screen of 1634 formed from a family pew. Some fragmentary medieval glass and several 20th-century windows by Hugh Powell.

⌃ HIGHCLERE 440603

St Michael

August 2003

Away from the village, on the Berkshire border south of Newbury. Rebuilt on a new site by George Gilbert Scott 1869-70, but retaining many monuments, notably to Richard Kingsmill, d.1600, with family effigies, and to Thomas, Earl of Pembroke, d.1740, carved by Roubiliac. Font, pulpit etc, also by Scott. Stained glass windows by Hardman, Powell and Kempe. The previous church plan is marked out (but overgrown) just north-west of Highclere Castle at SU 444589.

▼ HINTON ADMIRAL   213959

St Michael

July 2005

North-east of Christchurch on A35. Brick, built 1786 as a chapel to Christchurch. Tower classical. Remainder altered and 'Gothicized' by George Edmund Street 1875, and enlarged 1883.

▲ HINTON AMPNER   597276

All Saints

July 2006

East of Winchester on the Petersfield road. Of Saxon origin, as confirmed by 'long-and-short' work in the north-east and south-east quoins of the nave, but disguised by alterations to chancel in 13th century and 1844. Nave extended to west by Capel Tripp.1879-80, with a fancy rectangular turret. Twin east windows with glass by Patrick Reyntiens. Several 17th-century and later memorials and brasses to Stewkley family.

HOLDENHURST

Formerly in Hampshire, is now in Dorset.

⩔ HOLYBOURNE 732412

Holy Rood

March 2002

Beside the Holy Bourne's source in a picturesque north-east neighbour of Alton. Nave probably 12th-century, chancel 13th-century, north arcade 15th-century but aisle widened 1879. Spire of 1902 on earlier tower. Good nave roof and carved stone corbels, early 15th-century. Large benefactions board of 1784.

⩔ HORDLE SZ 274951

All Saints

October 2000

A little west of Lymington. Rebuilt 1872 by C.E. Giles in red brick. Its predecessor of 1830 succeeded the ruinous medieval chapel subservient to Milford at Hordle Cliff to the south (the graveyard still exists at SZ 264923 approx.). A projected tower with tall spire never progressed further than the capped-off stump. Mosaic reredos by Salviati.

∀ HOUGHTON 341326

All Saints

July 1995

On the Test, south of Stockbridge. Nave early 12th-century. Arcades and aisles developed during 13th-century, but chancel arch 1882, with much other renewal throughout. Weatherboarded west bell-turret on wooden posts 15th-century. Furnishings including communion rail and pulpit mostly of 1882 by J. Oldrid Scott. A painting, Ecce Homo, may be by Albani, 17th-century.

∀ HOUND 470087

St Mary

August 2001

Close to Southampton Water, north of Hamble. A delightfully unpretentious little rural building. Thirteenth-century, with west bell-turret on posts inside. Simple chancel arch. Three-fold east window of 1959 by Patrick Reyntiens, with its vivid blues and greens a surprisingly agreeable addition to its old surroundings.

⚘ HUNTON 481396

St James

March 1960

Between Winchester and Whitchurch. A humble church on its own beside the Dever stream, once a chapel to Crawley. Attributed to c.1500, but nave south wall 18th-century brick and bell-turret relatively new. A few old monuments.

➢ HURSLEY 427253

All Saints

August 1943

On the Romsey to Winchester road. Tower 15th-century, no longer with its spire. Remainder rebuilt 1846-48 by J.P. Harrison for the vicar John Keble, leader of the Oxford ('High Church') Movement. Important stained glass of the same period by William Wailes to a scheme by William Butterfield. Brass memorial to Keble, d.1866. In the churchyard the brick mausoleum of the Heathcote family, 1797.

HURSTBOURNE PRIORS   439466

St Andrew

June 2018

South-west of Whitchurch on the Bourne rivulet. Chancel 13th-century, north chapel 16th-century and brick south chapel 18th-century. West parts including yellow brick tower 1870 in the then outdated neo-Norman style. Twelfth-century west doorway re-used, also chancel arch moved to north chapel. Tomb of Robert Oxenbridge, d.1574, with family effigies, recoloured.

HURSTBOURNE TARRANT   386530

St Peter

September 1999

North-west of Whitchurch, in a very attractive village. Low and spreading, mostly early 13th-century but with a fine Norman doorway. West bays added to nave and aisles in 14th century. Nave roof and bell-turret 15th-century (spire added 1897). Wall-paintings in north aisle. Two fonts, one 13th-century circular with eight attached columns, the other rough and probably Saxon.

⌄ IBSLEY 151097

St Martin

May 2001

A former chapel to Fordingbridge three miles to the south, built 1654 and rebuilt in brick 1832 by John Peniston. Deconsecrated 1986 and adapted as an art gallery. Big monument to Sir John Constable d.1627 and family, the busts of the latter arranged like grapes on a vine.

⌃ IDSWORTH 743141

St Hubert

October 1946

Not a parish church, but a chapel to Chalton. Between Petersfield and Havant, close to the Sussex border. Small, basically 12th-century, on a wide slope of the Downs, and chiefly important for its 14th-century wall-paintings in the chancel representing, for example, the Feast of Herod and a hunting scene with St Hubert. But notable too for the unspoiled interior with box pews, 15th-century font, and 17th-century pulpit, combined with other entirely appropriate woodwork introduced or altered early in the 20th century under the architect Harry Goodhart-Rendel.

ITCHEN ABBAS 534327

St John the Baptist

August 1943

On the Itchen between Winchester and Alresford. Rebuilt 1861-63 in neo-Norman style by William Coles. Genuine 12th-century chancel arch, also doorway re-set in north transept. Much stained glass by Lavers and Westlake.

ITCHEN STOKE 559324

St Mary

September 1993

Just west of Alresford. With the Churches Conservation Trust. Rebuilt 1865-66 by Henry Conybeare, like a scaled-down version of the Sainte-Chapelle in Paris. In 13th-century style but unequalled in the county for its elaborate and colourful 19th-century wall surfaces and furnishings. High open timber roof with stencilled patterns. Much wall-arcading, and window glass with coloured geometric patterns. Maze design in glazed tiles on floor of apse. Cast-iron scrollwork in seating and pulpit. Font with rich marble, enamel and gilding. Brass altar rail and lectern. From the previous church two early 16th-century brasses.

KILMESTON 591263

St Andrew

May 1992

East of Winchester, near the source of the Itchen. Formerly a chapel to Cheriton. 'Rebuilt' 1772 with addition of south aisle and 'restored' to 13th-century style 1865. Which parts, if any, are medieval, is uncertain. Bell-turret 1911. Baluster-shaped font probably 18th-century. East window glass by Hugh Powell 1965.

KIMPTON 281467

SS Peter and Paul

August 1994

Four miles west of Andover. Nave and chancel 13th-century. Transepts, south arcade and aisle 14th-century. South porch 18th-century. Tower of brick and flint 1837. Sixteenth-century altar table and good 14th-century gabled piscina. Small tomb-chest of Robert Thornburgh, d.1522, with engaging figures of family. Several other monuments of interest.

KINGSCLERE 525586

St Mary

June 1996

In the town centre, between Newbury and Basingstoke. Cruciform and largely early 12th-century but much altered 1848-49 and nevertheless retaining some Norman features such as the north doorway and parts of the tower above its massive arches. South chapel and arcade c.1200. Several large windows obviously 15th-century insertions. Twelfth-century font with 17th-century cover, 17th-century pulpit. A great variety of stained glass, including (in the north transept) a portrayal of the Derby winner Ormonde. Many 16th-century brasses and other monuments brought into south chapel.

⅄ KINGSLEY   778378

St Nicholas

October 1956

East of Alton, towards the Surrey border. The original church, largely rebuilt in brick 1778 and now only used as a burial chapel. End walls and east window probably still 14th-century (the east now whitened). Round font of unknown date.

Ⓐ   All Saints

788383

August 2018

The 'new' church, by J.H. and E. Dyer, 1875-76. Interior with unattractive patterning in contrasting brick colours.

ⱴ KINGS SOMBORNE 360310

SS Peter and Paul

June 2018

South of Stockbridge on the Romsey Road. Long, with 'catslide' roof over the whole. Much rebuilt 1886, but parts of chancel arch and of south arcade 13th-century and short side chapels 14th-century. Over-sized wooden bell-tower spanning a bay and a half of the nave. Some interesting incised crosses and inscriptions on north doorway and elsewhere. Big 12th-century font. Eighteenth-century communion rail. Canopied tomb with effigy of 13th-century priest. Finely engraved 14th-century brasses of twin figures on chancel floor; Pevsner calls them 'Tweedledum and Tweedledee', though they differ. Brilliant display of local needlework in kneelers, vestments etc.

Ⱡ KINGS WORTHY 493324

St Mary

August 1943

On the Itchen, close to the north of Winchester. Tower 13th-century, but remainder rebuilt 1864 by John Colson, with some re-used stonework. Prominent octagonal vestry. Fourteenth-century font.

KINSON

Formerly in Hampshire, is now in Dorset.

⌄ KNIGHTS ENHAM 362481

St Michael and All Angels

March 1962

In what is virtually a northern suburb of Andover. Small and typical, with flat ceiling and medieval rood beam but no chancel arch. Twelfth-century, with 13th-century arcade partly exposed in south wall. Porch 17th-century. Small 12th-century font. Communion rail 17th-century, also possibly the screen.

⌃ LAINSTON 442315

St Peter

May 2009

North-west of Winchester on the Stockbridge road. Substantial ruin of nave in grounds of Lainston House (now an hotel). Twelfth-century stonework of north and south doorways and 17th-century west window.

ⅴ LASHAM 676426

St Mary

August 1997

On high ground north-west of Alton. Rebuilt 1866 by Henry Woodyer. Curious drooping foliage carving on vestry doorway. Pulpit of 1933, with 17th-century canopy brought from Herriard. Fine glass by Hardman in east window.

ⅴ LAVERSTOKE 486489

St Mary

May 2018

A little east of Whitchurch, up the Test valley. Rebuilt 1892-96 by John Pearson at cost of Portal family, to replace the medieval church of which some remains exist in the grounds of Laverstoke House. On a commanding site but not one of his most successful. Outstandingly elaborate internal finishes and furnishings including rood screen and carved Bavarian-style reredos, Stained glass throughout by Clayton and Bell.

LECKFORD 374376

St Nicholas

June 1949

North of Stockbridge on Andover road. Twelfth-century chancel and 13th-century nave, all with later windows. Chancel arch 15th-century, much off-centre probably because there has been a north arcade to the nave, with aisle. Twelfth-century font. Some old woodwork, notably in the 17th-century chancel stalls, supposedly from an Italian convent.

LINKENHOLT 363581

St Peter

September 1999

Close to the Wiltshire and Berkshire borders, in the highest village in Hampshire. Rebuilt 1870-71 by William White, re-using the stonework of one window and the late Norman south doorway. Round font of similar date with typical zigzag ornament. Some interesting stained glass.

☗ LISS 771287

St Peter

September 1946

The old church three miles north-east of Petersfield, more or less abandoned after the new was built. Restored 2014-15 for use by the International Presbyterian Church and now in the care of St Peter's Trust. Mostly 13th-century including the three-bay south arcade, but the north wall is 15th-century and the aisle itself was rebuilt in 1903. South porch dated 1639, but the attractive upper part is relatively new. Font 15th-century. Some 18th-century memorials.

☖ St Mary 775279

July 2018

The new church of St Mary, built 1890-92 by Sir Arthur Blomfield in Early English style, but with stately west tower added by Sir Edward Maufe 1929-32 (therefore pre-dating his Guildford Cathedral). Stained glass in chancel by Kempe and Co. Sculpture of the Child Christ by Eric Gill, 1932.

ⅴ LITCHFIELD 461540

St James

January 1999

North of Whitchurch off A34. In a village churchyard carpeted with snowdrops in spring. Twelfth-century with arcades of early 13th-century aisles, of which the south was rebuilt 1874-75 by Henry Woodyer, and the north is still blocked. Irregularities in the window spacing and in the arcades have baffled attempts to date the earlier sequence of development. Unusually large aumbry or cupboard in east wall. Rough font of unknown antiquity. Screen probably early 17th-century in its lower parts, but upper by Woodyer.

⅄ LITTLE SOMBORNE 382327

All Saints

August 1993

South-east of Stockbridge. In care of Churches Conservation Trust. Very small, 11th-century with subsequent alterations, e.g. chancel added in 12th century and later removed, leaving a blocked arch. Evidence of former anchorite's cell once attached to north side.

LITTLETON   453329

St Catherine

August 1993

Engulfed in the north-west spread of Winchester. Small, early 12th-century, with north aisle added 1885-86. No tower or bell turret, just an opening in the west gable. Stone screen in chancel arch with unusual side openings, possibly of 17th century. Sturdy nave roof scientifically dated to c.1400. Good 12th-century square Purbeck marble font.

LOCKERLEY   298266

St John the Evangelist

June 2018

Four miles north-west of Romsey. Entirely rebuilt 1889-90 by John Colson. One very small Norman window built into south transept. In the porch the disused font bowl and two 18th-century memorials. A giant old yew overshadows the site of the old church on the north side. Near it a possibly ancient altar mensa on two piers.

⚔ LONGPARISH   426439

St Nicholas

June 2018

East of Andover on the river Test. Norman priest's doorway in south wall of chancel. Tower probably 16th-century. Otherwise mostly 13th-century, the chancel arch and main south doorway being particularly good examples of Early English. Changes by Henry Woodyer in 1840s and '50s include inappropriate belfry windows and clock face. Baluster-shaped early 18th-century font. Nativity east window by Morris and Co. after Edward Burne-Jones and several other windows of interest including a memorial to the aviator George Hawker V.C., d.1916, by Francis Skeat.

⚔ LONGSTOCK   358371

St Mary

June 2018

Another Test valley village, just upstream from Stockbridge. Rebuilt 1877-80 by William White on the plan of its predecessor, retaining merely a medieval coffin lid, a group of 13th-century floor tiles in the sanctuary, and 18th-century altar rails. Notable 19th-century chancel roof with carved angels. These and other woodwork from the Exeter workshop of Harry Hems.

LYMINGTON   SZ 322955

St Thomas

March 1993

Prominently in the High Street with tower of 1670 and big cupola. Otherwise apparently medieval outside, but internally Georgian in character with segmental plaster ceiling of 1720. Galleries of 1792-1811 on three sides, with Tuscan columns in pairs, under and above. Some monuments of the same period. North chapel late 13th-century. 'Baluster' font 18th-century.

LONG SUTTON   738474

All Saints

August 2002

North of Alton and west of Farnham. A former chapel to Crondall, early 13th-century with lancet-windowed chancel. South aisle added a little later, perhaps as a pilgrims' chapel – hence the porch unusually placed in the angle between so as to allow separate access. Bell-turret on four stout posts within the nave. Eighteenth-century altar rails. Twelfth-century 'tub' font. Massive chest of similar date to the building, probably the oldest in Hampshire.

LYNDHURST 298082

St Michael

June 1959

In a commanding position above the High Street, a complete rebuilding in the 1860s by William White. An idiosyncratic interpretation of early Gothic styles on an almost cathedral scale, using brickwork in various colours and patterns inside and out, further enlivened by skilled carving in, for example, the stone capitals of the arcades and musician angels amongst the roof timbers. A painting of the Wise and Foolish Virgins by Lord Leighton forms the reredos. The High Victorian decoration is not to everyone's taste, but the stained glass may well have more appeal. Not only is the east window by Edward Burne-Jones but others are by such well-known names as William Morris, Charles Kempe, Clayton and Bell, Dante Gabriel Rossetti and Ford Madox Brown. From the 18th-century church on the site is a memorial by John Flaxman to Sir Charles Jennings, d.1798. The churchyard grave of the 'Alice' of Alice in Wonderland is inscribed with her married name, Mrs Reginald Hargreaves.

MAPLEDURWELL 687510

St Mary

October 1956

A little east of Basingstoke. Basically 12th-century, but too much 'restored' in 1853. Fourteenth-century pointed barrel roof and later rather amusingly over-sized bell turret. A little 15th-century work incorporated in chancel screen. Interesting brass to John Tanner and family with early 16th-century figures in costume.

MARTIN 070196

All Saints

May 2001

Seven miles south-west of Salisbury and formerly in Wiltshire, but now in Hampshire. Twelfth-century nave, extended eastwards to form a bigger chancel and again with transepts in 14th century to form a cruciform plan. North transept further enlarged eastwards later to form an aisle. Tower 13th-century at base but upper part 15th-century and spire rebuilt in 18th century. Font 18th-century baluster-shaped.

MARTYR WORTHY 516327

St Swithun

August 1943

Just north-east of Winchester. Nave 12th-century with original doorways but later windows. Chancel neo-Norman, 1865. Bell-turret 1871. Good 14th-century roof over east part of nave. In the churchyard a ridged gravestone of around 1200, probably the oldest in the county.

⋎ MATTINGLEY 736580

No known dedication

October 1998

North of Odiham on the Reading road. A great surprise and a great rarity – a totally timber-framed church of somewhere about 1500 and quite domestic in character. Six-and-a-half bays with original oak posts supporting the fully braced roof. The aisles in the same style were added in 1867 by William Butterfield, and the timber porch moved from the south to north side. Panelled ceilings below the bellcote and above the altar. Seventeenth-century wall-panelling in sanctuary.

⋎ MEDSTEAD 654372

St Andrew

July 1995

Between Alresford and Alton, north of A31. Low north aisle hidden from the road, with 12th-century arcade. Chancel c.1400, though with lancet windows. Bell-turret 1860. Thirteenth-century stone foliage corbel used as a stand for the collecting box.

⋎ MEONSTOKE 612203

St Andrew

June 1946

By the Meon valley road north-east of Bishops Waltham. Picturesquely situated, with an attractive 15th-century timber-topped tower. Remainder 13th-century with roofs spreading over the nave and aisles. Square Norman font of Purbeck marble. Little 17th-century German carved wood panel of Jacob wrestling with an Angel.

⋏ MICHELDEVER 592391

St Mary

August 1994

Five miles north of Winchester. Massive stone tower of 1544, and behind it an octagonal brick nave boldly inserted in 1806-08 by George Dance into the middle of what had been a traditional aisled church. Beyond it the long chancel still is medieval, though altered in the 1880s. The nave is brilliantly lit with big plain high windows and ceiled with a star vault of plaster — all astonishing at first encounter. It is interesting to find the remains of the former 13th-century arcades, cut short where the octagon was inserted, and to compare the shape with Dance's other eight-sided church, that of St Bartholomew-the-Less in London (1789). Several good memorials to the Baring family, his sponsors at Micheldever, and a wall-tablet outside to Benjamin Whitaker, d.1751, Chief Justice of South Carolina. Many large monuments in the churchyard too.

⌄ MICHELMERSH 346266

St Mary

March 1993

North of Romsey in the Test valley. Timber tower, completely weatherboarded, and originally detached from the early 13th-century church. Short chapels each side of chancel. Most unusual 13th-century font with heads under corners of bowl, lilies between them, and 17th-century wall-panelling around 14th-century knight's effigy with angels by his pillow and his feet against a stag.

⌃ MILFORD-ON-SEA SZ 291922

All Saints

March 1993

South-west of Lymington, by the southern tip of the present county. An almost wholly 13th-century church, once cruciform with a central tower. Earlier round arches to south arcade, the first three bays up to where a central tower was. Transepts merged into aisle extensions. Tower rebuilt at west end in 13th century leaving what Pevsner calls 'a very botched job' at the former crossing, in spite of an attractive 17th-century roof over that area. Good south doorway and porch. Modern parish room on north side.

➢ MILLBROOK 385132

Holy Trinity

May 2004

Two miles west of Southampton city centre. Totally rebuilt 1873-80 by Henry Woodyer to replace the already decrepit former St Nicholas', which eventually collapsed in 1920. Its site lies under the dual carriageway A33. The successor is far more urban in character, without any departure from the then fashionable Early English version of Gothic. The best feature is the 1920 War Memorial chapel in the south aisle, with an altarpiece by Sir Ninian Comper. He also designed the great baldacchino over the main altar.

⚲ MILTON SZ 237944

St Mary Magdalen

October 2000

Between Christchurch and Lymington. An early 17th-century brick tower, dwarfed by the church of 1831 behind it attributed to William Hiscock. The east end was extended laterally in 1928 by Sir Howard Robertson and a four-bay north aisle added in 1958 by Sebastian Comper. The adjoining hall is of 1932. Monument to Thomas White, d.1720, called 'irresistibly funny' by Pevsner because the omission of his kneeling legs in the confined space contrasts with his pompous costume and the faces of the accompanying cherubs.

⋎ MINSTEAD 281109

All Saints

September 1962

In the New Forest, two miles north-west of Lyndhurst, with not only the rural charm, outside and within, but also the evidence of woodworking skills that one would expect from its surroundings. Thirteenth-century walling in the chancel and its arch, overwhelmed by a complex array of galleries shoehorned in to accommodate as many pews as possible, and augmented by big 18th-century transepts – the south for the squire and his family and the north formerly a schoolroom. One family pew at floor level has a fireplace. Nearly all windows are domestic in character. Brick tower of 1774 and porch of 1683. Square font late 12th-century with figure carvings. 'Three-decker' pulpit, not elaborate.

⋏ MONK SHERBORNE 608558

All Saints

February 2002

Three miles north-west of Basingstoke. Mostly 12th-century, with large north doorway and wide chancel arch. Fourteenth century chancel windows. Nineteenth-century bell-turret on older substructure. Alongside it a stair-turret perhaps meant as the start of a tower, also a large 14th-century porch that was apparently once a lychgate. Font partly 13th-century with three strange heads under the bowl. Pulpit of 1651, a rare Cromwell-era date. A variety of stained glass, including in the vestry what Pevsner calls 'a sweetly inept set'.

∀ MONXTON 313446

St Mary

May 1999

Three miles west of Andover on the Roman Port Way. Completely rebuilt by Henry Woodyer 1852-53, re-using the chancel arch capitals and the bell-frame. Nice brass of 1599 with figures of Alice Swayne and her son.

∧ MORESTEAD 510255

No dedication

December 1991

Three miles south-east of Winchester, also on a Roman road. Twelfth-century in origin but much renewed, and only the north and inner south doorways are ancient. Wide neo-Norman chancel arch. The building of 1833 against the west end was the village schoolroom. Font probably Norman.

⌄ MOTTISFONT 326267

St Andrew

May 1993

In the Test valley, north of Romsey. Twelfth-century with a fine Norman chancel arch, but windows mostly 14th- and 15th-centuries. Uncommon amount of 15th-century glass in chancel, notably in the tracery of the east window. An interesting monument of 1584 with family figures kneeling in a row.

⌃ NATELY SCURES 697530

St Swithun

August 1943

On A30 between Basingstoke and Odiham. Tiny Norman, with only a farm for company. No chancel arch, but a beautifully rounded apse, the kind of east termination that in most churches was soon replaced with something grander. Trefoil-headed north doorway, most unusual for its 12th-century date. Rare too is a mermaid carving on one (replica) capital. Little 19th-century gallery on a much older beam. More memorials than one would expect the space to allow, including a brass to Thomas Carleton, d.1817, a Governor of New Brunswick, a tablet to his son, and others shaped like the four playing-card symbols.

⋀ NETHER WALLOP 304364

St Andrew

August 1943

Off A30, west of Stockbridge, on the flank of a steep hill. Remarkable for the oldest known wall-paintings in England - over the former chancel arch two flying angels of the early 11th century, in the style of carvings and illuminated manuscripts of that period. Aisles added to 11th-century nave in 13th century and chancel arch made higher. Aisles next extended further east and in due course widened to the extent of former transepts. Present chancel and arch 1845. Tower rebuilt 1704, with 13th-century arch. Good low-pitched 15th-century roofs. More wall-paintings, mainly in the nave, are 15th-century. St George and the Dragon, and Christ with trade emblems. A fine 15th-century brass to a prioress of Amesbury and in the churchyard the big pyramidal tomb of Francis Douce, 'Doctor of Physick', d.1760.

⋎ NEW ALRESFORD 589326

St John the Baptist

July 1946

The 'new' town was founded in 1200 by the Bishop of Winchester and severely damaged by fire in 1689. After that the church was virtually rebuilt, including the plain brick top of the 14th-century tower. The rest of it was extensively rebuilt again in 1896-98 by Sir Arthur Blomfield. Bits of 13th- and 14th-century work can still be detected in the tower base and elsewhere. From the 18th century some memorial tablets and churchyard tombs. Also in the churchyard some headstones to French prisoners of war of the Napoleonic era.

⌄ NEWNHAM 704540

St Nicholas

September 1956

East of Basingstoke, to the north of A30. Uninspiring rebuilding of 1847 by Benjamin Thorne, his tower cap a variant on the Rhenish helm type (cf. Hawkley). But two doorways and the chancel arch are 12th-century, and communion rails early 18th-century.

⌃ NEWTON VALENCE 724328

St Mary

September 1998

Four miles south of Alton. Basically 13th-century but much renewed 1871 by Sir Arthur Blomfield. Tower top of brick, 1812. East window of three stepped lancets under one arch, and below it the empty niches of a late 15th-century reredos. Monuments to Captain Robert Nicholas, 'lost in a hurricane off the island of Hispaniola' in 1780, and Audrey Lempriere, died at Sebastopol 1855. One of the church bells is 14th-century with an inscription in English rather than the usual Latin.

⩔ NORTH BADDESLEY   402208

St John

August 1943

Between Romsey and Eastleigh, an unspoiled gem in open country well to the north of the present village. Nave perhaps 12th- or 13th-century but with some later brickwork. Chancel 15th-century. Varied windows, that on south-east of nave with angel carvings, 14th-century. Curiously small tower of 1674 and wood-framed porch of similar date. The interior retains a feeling of the 17th century too with its pulpit and balustered screen (dated 1602). West gallery renewed, but with an early 19th-century casement window to light it. Simple font 14th-century. Fifteenth-century tomb-chest of a Knight Hospitaller in the chancel, also a big monument to John More, d.1620.

⩔ NORTH HAYLING   730032

St Peter

August 1970

One of the two medieval churches on the island, informal and inviting. The shingled belfry stands, unusually, over the east bay of the nave. The 12th-century chancel (on the left of the sketch) is heavily buttressed. The rest, including north and south arcades and aisles, is mostly 13th-century, the north transept being slightly later. Tapered 'tub' font, 13th-century. Some neat early 19th-century memorials to Rogers and Bannister families, and in the churchyard a particularly fine array of 18th- and early 19th-century headstones.

➢ NORTHINGTON 564374

St John the Evangelist

August 1943

North-west of Alresford in the Candover valley, rebuilt 1887-90 by Sir Thomas Jackson in East Anglian Perpendicular style with flint flushwork, yet with a commanding Somerset-type tower. North aisle and French-style east end. Interior altogether less interesting - the spired turret on the south side is merely for a pulpit stair. Monuments to the 1st Earl of Northbrook, d.1786, and the Baring family, the latter of 1848 by Richard Westmacott the younger.

⋎ NORTH STONEHAM 441174

St Nicholas

August 1993

North of Southampton, in a narrow green belt short of Eastleigh. The three gables and square-topped aisle windows are reminiscent of Devon or Cornwall, and actually the church is of 1590 to 1610, an unusual time for such rebuilding. The chancel arcades, north and south, are believed to be at least in part of that period, but those of the nave may be medieval. The window stonework presents similar puzzles to experts, a triple-lancet window in the west wall being clearly a 13th-century one re-used. New vestry 2008. Some interesting monuments include the tomb of Sir Thomas Fleming, d.1613, with effigies, and a marble memorial to Admiral Lord Hawke, d.1781, with a detailed relief of the battle of Quiberon Bay. On the chancel floor is the gravestone of Slavonian sailors who died at Southampton in 1491.

⋎ NORTH WALTHAM 560465

St Michael

August 1994

Five miles south-west of Basingstoke, close to A30. Rebuilt 1865-66 by John Colson, retaining most of the north arcade and some other 12th-century stonework. Fourteenth-century piscina and 15th-century font. East window glass dismissed by Pevsner's successor as 'terrible'.

⋎ NURSLING 359165

St Boniface

August 2007

In a little non-industrial oasis four miles north-west of Southampton, too close to M27 and M271. Early 14th-century, probably with a Saxon core. A long-vanished monastery nearby was the starting-point of the eighth-century St Boniface who evangelised Germany. Timber steeple over south porch, taller than most others in the county. Thirteenth-century south transept containing the fine canopied tomb of Sir Richard Mille, d.1613, and a big decorative tablet to Thomas Knollys, d.1751. Nice Jacobean pulpit.

NUTLEY 609445

St Mary

August 1943

South of Basingstoke on the road to the Candovers. The church was rebuilt in 1845 and demolished in 1955, 12 years after this pencil sketch, made when it was evidently already disused.

OAKLEY 567504

St Leonard

February 2002

Four miles west of Basingstoke, near the Whitchurch road. Rebuilt 1868-70 by Thomas Wyatt, adding the north aisle and keeping much of the older stonework. This includes the 14th-century tower arch, early 16th-century west doorway and south aisle windows. The south arcade starts with a scalloped capital of late Norman type and ends with a panelled arch of c.1500. Tower stair turret with interesting ornamentation inside, due to Wyatt. Font thought to be the base of a standing Cross, turned upside-down. A brass memorial is to the parents of an archbishop, Robert Warham, d.1487, and his wife. Alabaster effigies of early 16th-century knight and lady on tomb-chest with tiny angels by their pillows.

⌃ ODIHAM 740509

All Saints

October 1956

Between Basingstoke and Farnham, a town church in an ample churchyard. Prominent west tower embraced by wide aisles, 13th-century in the ground storey but otherwise of 1649 in red brick, ornamented with Ionic pilasters – large at the angles and small flanking all the belfry windows. Nave arcades very tall for Hampshire, the north of three bays late 15th-century but the south of four bays probably a 17th-century reconstruction of a 14th-century one. Chancel arcades very different, shorter and early 13th-century. Unusual doorway in east wall, now blocked, probably led to a vestry. Late 12th-century pillar piscina in chancel. west gallery 1836, a two-part re-making of the 17th-century one. Communion rail in north chapel 18th-century. Pulpit 1634. Royal arms of 1660 over chancel arch with unusual motto 'Beati Pacifici', 'Blessed are the Peacemakers'. Two strongly coloured abstract windows by Patrick Reyntiens. Many brasses of 15th to 17th centuries. Several later tablets, including two outside to French officers of Napoleon's time.

⌄ OLD ALRESFORD 588336

St Mary

July 1946

One mile north of New Alresford, beyond the dam built c.1200 across the Arle. Small medieval chancel, and long brick nave of 1753, later refaced with flint and brick banding. Robust west tower, also of brick, 1769. South transept added 1858 by John Colson. Jacobean altar-table. Several monuments of note, the finest being to Jane, Lady Rodney, d.1757, with bust and figures of Faith and Hope. In the churchyard are a number of early 19th-century chest-tombs and the granite temple-like mausoleum of C.E.G. Schwerdt, d.1939, by Sebastian Comper.

⋎ OTTERBOURNE   465226

St Matthew

May 1970

On A33, south of Winchester. What was left of the old church was the ruin of the 13th-century chancel, close to the railway and the waters of the Itchen. It was demolished in the year after my sketch.

⋎   St Matthew   56228

April 2018

The successor church of 1837-39, a half-mile to the west of the old, designed by the squire W.C. Yonge, father of Charlotte Yonge the novelist. Apse and north aisle added 1875. Yonge's clumsy bell-turret originally had a spire, which became unsafe. But his steep-pitched nave roof is a fine piece of carpentry with prominently cusped arches. Communion rail late 17th-century, apparently from 'an abbey in Flanders'.

⋁ OVERTON 515500

St Mary

August 1994

On the Test, east of Whitchurch. Much renewed 1850-54 by Benjamin Ferrey, but retaining an interesting amount of medieval work. Three bays of north and south arcades c.1200 with round columns and scalloped capitals. Chancel 13th-century. Roofs of both nave and chancel c.1300. West tower 1538, along with west bays of arcades, but again rebuilt 1908. Double-leaf south door probably of 1538 too. East window of chancel a fine example of the work of Charles Kempe, 1903, A wall-tablet to Thomas Streatwells, 'silk throwster' and one of the founders of the town's silk mill. Church room added 1999, linked to north aisle.

The little former chapel at Quidhampton a half-mile to the north-east (518504) has long been used only for farm purposes. 'Herring-bone' walling clearly shows its early Norman origin.

⋀ OVER WALLOP 284383

St Peter

March 1962

South-west of Andover, near the Wiltshire border. Much renewed 1865-74 by John Pearson, considered a good example of his conservation and restoration of medieval work. Arcades variously 13th- and 14th-centuries, the earlier with round arches. The font is 15th-century but the roof and most other fittings are Pearson's. They include a wrought-iron pulpit and screen panels.

⌄ OVINGTON 562316

St Peter

June 2018

On the Itchen, just west of Alresford, the first church I had ever been taken to by electric car (driven by my son)! Completely rebuilt 1866-67 by John Colson. The *Buildings of England* notes 'Colson's usual naturalistic carving and a prettily painted chancel roof'. The square 12th-century font survives, and in the churchyard the stonework of a doorway as well as the classical sarcophagus of Sir Thomas Dyer, d.1838. His hatchment with flags is in the church.

⋀ OWSLEBURY 515234

St Andrew

December 1991

Between Winchester and Bishops Waltham. Chancel 13th-century. Tower dated 1675, and the nave and aisles may be partly of that period, judging by the gabled windows of the aisles. But the columns were of iron and were encased in wood, and augmented, in 1956. Wall-panelling in the nave made up from Jacobean pews. Communion rail 18th-century. Fine monument with obelisk and urns to Lord Carpenter, d.1749.

⚐ PAMBER 608581

Holy Trinity, Our Lady and St John the Baptist

January 2002

Six miles north-west of Basingstoke. This was a Benedictine priory, founded early in the 12th century but dissolved in 1414. The massive central tower and long chancel of the cruciform church still stand and are used. The nave has gone, though the position of its west wall can be traced, as well as the extent of the cloister on its south side. Very fine triple lancet east windows. Blocked arches to north and south led to east chapels of the transepts, which have disappeared. Traces of 15th-century paintings on the nave walls. Chancel screen and font also 15th-century. Monuments include a 12th-century foliated coffin lid and a rare oak effigy of a 14th-century knight.

⚐ PEAR TREE GREEN 440118

Jesus

May 2004

In a suburb of Southampton ('St Mary Extra') on the east bank of the Itchen, Jesus Chapel, founded in 1618 as a chapel to St Mary's in Southampton, and believed to be the first new church built in England after the Reformation. Foundation stone over west arch of nave, the only original part remaining. Various extensions from 1622 onwards have left the interior a rather incoherent shape, but with a wealth of monuments of the early 19th century. Several are by such well known sculptors as Henry Westmacott and Sir Francis Chantrey.

⌄ PENTON MEWSEY 330474

Holy Trinity

August 1994

Close to the north-west of Andover. A small and little-altered building of about 1370, even with its two bells in the original bellcote. Fine window tracery, especially the curvilinear pattern of the west window. Nave roof largely of the same date, also an ogee-arched piscina in the south wall where a side altar was. Font 14th-century too. Eighteenth-century communion rail with twisted balusters.

◄ PETERSFIELD 746232

St Peter

May 2004

A Norman town church with an unusually interesting history of development. Though only as a chapel to neighbouring Buriton, it was begun early in the 12th century as an ambitious cruciform building with a central tower. With a change of policy in the middle of the century a west tower was built. As much of the crossing tower as had been built was taken down, all but its sumptuous east arch (now the chancel arch). Linking north and south arcades were formed, still round arched, and the aisles widened to the extent of the former transepts. Much was changed in the 18th century, and again in 1873-74 by Sir Arthur Blomfield. He altered the arcades, added the clerestory, and rebuilt the chancel. A variety of stained glass, and an assembly of 18th- and 19th-century wall-tablets. My picture is based on a water-colour reproduced on cards for sale to visitors.

ꓦ PLAITFORD 278203

St Peter

February 2001

On the Southampton to Salisbury road, formerly in Wiltshire but now in Hampshire. Much rebuilt in 19th century, but retaining the north and south doorways. Medieval floor tiles on sanctuary wall.

ꓦ PORTCHESTER 625045

St Mary

August 1985

At the head of Portsmouth harbour. Within the area of a big Roman fort, once a cruciform priory church, a splendid example.of Norman architecture with very little alteration or restoration. West front with richly ornamented doorway and windows, a remarkable survival. Arcades and tower arches of equal quality, with ornament of late Norman character verging on the Gothic. The south transept has gone, and the chancel was curtailed about 1600, but the latter still shows the remains of wall-arcading that once ran round most of the east parts. Magnificent round font 12th-century too, with intersecting arches under a fascinating pattern of birds, beasts and foliage reminiscent of Celtic ornament. Communion rail possibly Elizabethan. On the north wall an ornate board commemorating the funding of repairs after a fire in 1705 and displaying the largest church Royal arms in the county. Monument to Sir Thomas Cornwallis, died 1618, by the celebrated sculptor Nicholas Stone.

⌄ St George 634002

March 1959

Close to the Portsmouth Harbour railway station. Built in brick 1754, probably designed by a surveyor to the nearby dockyard. A cruciform shape within a square, defined inside by four tall columns. Exterior two-storied to light the galleries, with a third storey on the west front and an elegant bell-turret – all rather reminiscent of New England. Badly damaged by bombing, and restored, so little of its period survives inside.

⌃ PORTSEA 652008

St Mary

October 1964

In Fratton Road, centrally in Portsea Island. On a medieval site, partly rebuilt 1843 and again wholly in 1887-89 under Sir Arthur Blomfield. On a grand scale in the Perpendicular style that had by then become fashionable to imitate. A long tall open interior with hammer-beam roof. Elaborate reredos and giant pulpit. Stained glass 'in rather sickly colours' by Burlison and Grylls. Crucifixion painting in south-east chapel attributed to Flemish school.

➤ PORTSMOUTH 632993

Cathedral of St Thomas of Canterbury

March 1959

I first visited this as a Naval rating from Leydene in 1946, never imagining that twelve years later I would become heavily involved as assistant architect in connection with maintenance and what turned out to be an abortive scheme to complete it – nor that I would be married there. The view reproduced here endured throughout the Second World War and for many years after, and became extremely familiar. The building of a power station so close would nowadays be unthinkable. Its chimney contrasted oddly with the gaunt brick wall that marked the closing down of building work in 1939. Neither now exists.

The building history can be briefly summarised a follows: Chapel in parish of St Mary Portsea founded c.1185 following the murder of St Thomas in Canterbury (now the aisled eastern Chapel of St Thomas with transeptal chapels, a fine example of the Early English style); became parish church 1320; nave (present quire) rebuilt in 1680s, some decades after damage in Civil War, also tower in new position at west end; became Cathedral 1927; extensions by Sir Charles Nicholson 1935-9, comprising outer aisles to quire, additional transepts north and south of tower, three bays of an entirely new nave with inner and outer aisles, and a 'cloister' range of vestries etc. to the north; completion of nave 1990-91 by Michael Drury with one further matching bay, twin western towers, ambulatory and west front – all in faultless harmony with Nicholson's work, albeit less ambitious.

Tower cupola early 18th-century with replica 'Golden Barque' weather vane (the original is exhibited inside). Bronze west doors by Bryan Kneale. Pulpit of 1693. Much of the choir seating 17th- and 18th-century work, though rearranged. Quire organ case by Abraham Jordan, 1718, nave organ case by Didier Grassin and Patrick Caulfield, 2001. Fifteenth-century font of standard type, augmented by large new one beneath tower. Ceramic plaque of Virgin and Child by Andrea della Robbia. Many 17th-century and later monuments, including the imposing one to the Duke of Buckingham, murdered nearby in 1628.

∨ Garrison Church of St John and St Nicholas 633993
March 1959

In Old Portsmouth. Not really within the criteria of this book as it was never parochial. Much like St Mary's Hospital in Chichester, the 'Domus Dei' was built in the second quarter of the 13th century to accommodate the sick and aged, and only the east part was a chapel. After the Reformation it became a military store, but in 1866 it was restored as a church by George Street, and is still an important example of the Early English style, even though the nave and aisles were left an eloquent shell by the bombs of 1940. Vaulted chancel with first-rate foliage carving in bosses and corbels. Craftsmanship resembling that of the contemporary east aisles of the nearby Cathedral. Effective 'Ascension' east window glass by Carl Edwards, 1958.

∨ Dockyard Church of St Ann 632006
November 2001

Also not a parish church, built for Dockyard officials and staff, originally (1704) on a different site. Rebuilt in 1785-86, probably by the Admiralty surveyor and perhaps with help from Thomas Telford over the design. A plain brick rectangle, shortened by one bay after war damage. Light elegant interior. Gracefully curved gallery on three sides with Royal arms thought to have been on an 18th-century Admiral's barge. Ornamented flat ceiling survived the bombing.

∀ St Mary   507451

September 2010

From one extreme of height to the other - the 'new' church of 1884-85 by Sir Arthur Blomfield, on a new site a little north-east of the old. Unusually large flint facings. Shingled spire. Interior of stone and brick. The glass of the east window by Heaton, Butler and Bayne has been commended.

∧ PRESTON CANDOVER   604414

St Mary

August 1943

A few miles north of Alresford. The old church, of which only the late 12th-century chancel survives, with scant remains of 18th-century wall-painting, several attractive wall-tablets and 17th-century communion rails. Now in the care of Churches Conservation Trust, the churchyard grass being kept under control economically by members of a local flock.

⬥ PRIORS DEAN 728296

Dedication unknown

June 1946

Between Petersfield and Alton, delightfully hidden in rural surroundings and in care of Churches Conservation Trust. Small early 12th-century with little Victorian bell-turret supported on four heavy medieval posts within the nave. Chancel arch and inappropriate lancet windows 19th-century too. But monuments more numerous than one would expect, including many of the 17th century.

◄ PRIVETT 676270

Holy Trinity

February 2008

North-west of Petersfield, in sight of the Winchester road. Rebuilt by Sir Arthur Blomfield in 1876-78 on an urban scale far in excess of the needs of the small village. Now in care of Churches Conservation Trust, and a conspicuous landmark in spite of so many tall trees encircling it. With no hint of departures from strict Early English style and outstanding for the quality of the stonework and of the carpentry of the roof. Fine furnishings too, and stained glass mostly by Heaton, Butler and Bayne. Wall-tablet to the benefactor William Nicholson, died 1909.

▼ QUARLEY 272439

St Michael

April 1958

Five miles west of Andover. Nave 11th-century, with typically Saxon 'herring-bone' masonry in north wall, and thin stones forming arches to two windows. No bell-cote: three bells hung in a detached wooden frame from which two have been stolen. East window believed to be one of the earliest of Venetian pattern (triple with the central one round-arched) in England. Altar table ingeniously made with the crown of an old yew supporting a Purbeck marble mensa. Twelfth-century 'tub' font. Seventeenth-century domestic stair balusters incorporated into pulpit and communion rail.

▲ RINGWOOD 145054

SS Peter and Paul

December 1993

On the Avon, close to the Dorset border. Completely rebuilt 1853-55 by F. and H. Francis. Straightforward Early English to Decorated in style. Pevsner calls the chancel 'quite splendid' with its closely-set lancet windows. Thirteenth-century double piscina from the previous church, also 18th-century brass chandelier and two 17th-century 'architectural' monuments.

▲ ROCKBOURNE 116184

St Andrew

September 1956

Three miles north-west of Fordingbridge. Originally cruciform Norman, but no longer with central tower. North transept and its arch 12th-century, south transept absorbed into south aisle, with 13th-century arcade. Timber-framed tower dated 1613 at west end of aisle. Porch of 1893. Early 16th-century triptych from Dutch school of painting. Early 19th-century memorials to Coote family.

➤ ROMSEY   351213

St Laurence (Parish)

April 2018

Romsey Abbey church (unlike Netley for example) can be included here not so much for its completeness but because in part or as a whole it has served the parish since the Middle Ages (when the Abbey was dissolved it was sold to the town for £100). The monastery was founded for nuns in 907 and their church began to be replaced by the present one about 1120. Building of the whole east end, the arches of the central tower, and the transepts progressed from then till about 1150. The four east bays of the nave are of later in the 12th century and the remaining three bays were finished about 1230. All the convent buildings as well as the eastern Lady Chapel have been demolished. Inside the church the building phases can be traced from east to west, with changes as work progressed – e.g. the giant columns at the start of the nave that then gave way to more normal ones, and the adoption of Gothic pointed arches towards the west end as seen in the sketch. The stumpy tower probably never went any higher. Many of the furnishings are 19th-century but the following are notable: large early 16th-century reredos painting in north transept; 16th-century Flemish wooden chest with intricate 'flamboyant' carving; small Saxon crucifix in south-east chapel, and another much more impressive on outside wall of south transept; in the south transept a 13th-century woman's effigy under ornamental canopy, also a 17th-century monument with coloured busts of John St Barbe and wife, and the grave slab of Earl Mountbatten, d.1979; in the nave a late 19th-century figure of a sleeping child, carved by her doctor father. Much of the window glass is by Charles Kempe or Clayton and Bell.

▼ ROPLEY 646320

St Peter

August 1977

Three miles east of Alresford. Much rebuilt 1896 by John Oldrid Scott, but retaining the 14th-century arcade to the south chapel, two doorways (one Norman) and 17th-century porch. Fifteenth-century font. The whole church was gutted by fire in June 2014 and will soon be reconstructed with a single roof covering the entire congregational area, an extension on the north side with kitchen, lavatories etc., and the tower on the south side rebuilt on its old foundations.

▼ ROTHERWICK 712563

Dedication unknown

October 1998

North-west of Odiham and beyond Hook. Nave unusually timber-framed with brick facing, like some modern houses. Wood structure including roof 15th-century, but brickwork 16th-century. Tower all brick, early 18th-century. Flint-faced chancel c.1300. North aisle and chapel 1876. Good glass in a north window by Geoffrey Robinson, 1962. Imposing monument to Frederick Tylney, died 1725. Much smaller tablet to Anthony More, died 1583, with amusing painted mermaid.

⋎ ROWNER 582017

St Mary

September 2003

An old village church set amongst tall trees, but swamped by housing estates between Fareham and Gosport. Against its west end a very large extension was added in 1965 by Potter and Hare. From its interior one sees two arches with altar between. The right arch frames the tiny old building, the left one its former north aisle which was widened in 1874 so as to create a bigger nave. Between them the 13th-century arcade still stands. A piscina was moved back to the original chancel. Amongst numerous monuments are a tomb-chest of 1559 to a member of the Brune family and a brass to John Castleman, died 1778, with delicate ornament.

⋎ ST MARY BOURNE 423503

St Peter

September 1999

Three miles north-west of Whitchurch. Notable for its fine Decorated chancel with low wide 12th-century arch and for its spacious 12th-century nave. But the nave arcades are a puzzle to historians because the columns are seriously out of alignment – probably because the spacing on the south side was dictated by an earlier tower there. That was superseded by the existing 15th- and 16th-century tower which awkwardly cuts off the end of the north arcade. Splendid large 12th-century font of black Tournai marble, very like those in Winchester Cathedral and at East Meon. Fine late 17th-century lectern with four-sided book-rest. Communion rail early 17th-century. Painted texts of the same period on south chapel wall and faintly in nave. In the churchyard a very ancient yew and a wealth of table-tombs.

▼ SELBORNE 741338

St Mary

July 1946

South-east of Alton. Mostly 12th-century, restored 1856-83 by William White, great-nephew of the local naturalist Gilbert White. Scalloped capitals and pointed arches, and thus Transitional in style. Chancel 13th-century. North transept a 14th-century chantry chapel. Communion rail 16th-century, brought from St Juliot in Cornwall. Triptych altar painting of the Adoration attributed to 16th-century painter Mostaert and regarded as 'outstandingly good'. Two windows commemorating Gilbert White: one of 1920 by H. Hinckes showing all the 82 species of birds mentioned by White. Tablet to White's grandfather Gilbert, died 1728.

▲ SHALDEN 693416

SS Peter and Paul

August 1997

North-west of Alton. Entirely rebuilt 1864-65 by John Colson. Font 15th-century. Spirited stained glass by Hardman.

⋏ SHERBORNE ST JOHN 624556

St Andrew

February 2002

A little north of Basingstoke. Twelfth-century nave and 13th-century chancel. North aisle added 1854, but north (Brocas) chapel early 15th-century, with 18th-century brick alterations. South porch also brick, dated 1533. Tower probably 14th-century at base, but upper part and spire 1834. Fifteenth-century roof, partly panelled. Square Purbeck marble font 12th-century, with 17th-century cover. Communion rail late 17th-century. Canopied pulpit dated 1634. Three-sided lectern late 17th-century. Stained glass from various sources collected in Brocas chapel. Fine collection of memorials in the chapel, mostly to Brocas family, including brasses from 14th century onwards and later tablets. Pevsner singled out the framed alabaster bust of Richard Atkins, died 1635 and, more prominently, the early 16th-century tomb of Ralph Pexall and wife that occupies the arch to the chapel.

⋎ SHERFIELD ENGLISH 291224

St Leonard

March 1960

Four miles west of Romsey on the Salisbury road. Poorly rebuilt 1858 on a site a quarter-mile south of the medieval church, but again in 1902 with no expense spared, by the little-known architect Fred Bath. His tower with flying buttresses to the corner pinnacles is loosely based on the far more elegant Fotheringhay in Northamptonshire. Stained glass of Art Nouveau character, i.e. contemporary with the building. Pulpit with 17th-century panels, possibly Dutch. From the old church the 18th-century font cover and communion rail.

⋀ SHERFIELD-ON-LODDON   672568

St Leonard

June 2018

Four miles north-east of Basingstoke, away from the village. Little of interest left after 1865-76 'restoration'. Some medieval stonework, such as the 14th-century east window of which the tracery is nevertheless much renewed. Overpowering tower and spire 1871-72 by J.W. Hugall. Some 16th-century glass in two nave windows, and plenty of 19th-century by Clayton and Bell and others. Two 16th-century brasses.

⌄ SHIPTON BELLINGER   233454

St Peter

August 1994

West of Andover on the Wiltshire border. Basically 13th- and 14th-centuries but largely rebuilt 1877-79, with some doorway and window stonework retained. East and west window glass of that date by Daniel Bell. Stone chancel screen partly medieval.

SILCHESTER 643623

St Mary

September 1999

North of Basingstoke on Berkshire border, the church being just within the former east gate of the extensive Roman town of Calleva Atrebatum. Indeed, a rough Roman wall forms the east boundary of the churchyard. Nave 12th-century, north arcade only slightly later, and the south arcade and chancel slightly later still, perhaps c.1230. South aisle rebuilt in 14th century. Fifteenth-century bell-turret on stout posts, and various minor changes that have left it unspoiled. Thirteenth-century wall-paintings in chancel. Original 14th-century grisaille glass in east window of north aisle. Fourteenth-century font with hanging iron corona of 1985. Splendid canopied pulpit dated 1639. Early 16th-century screen with pomegranate emblems of Katharine of Aragon. Fourteenth-century woman's effigy within big recess in south aisle. Two good 18th-century memorial tablets. Also two sadly weathered 13th-century coffin lids outside the south aisle.

SOBERTON 609168

SS Peter and Paul

June 1946

In the Meon valley, three miles east of Bishops Waltham. A church exhibiting slow growth from a Saxon or Norman nucleus. North and south arcades late 12th- and early 13th-century respectively in their two eastern bays, but evidence of later lengthening westward, and of an earlier tower being replaced by the present one in the 15th century. South transept and chancel late 13th-century and chancel rebuilt in 14th century. In the little altered south transept are extensive wall-paintings of c.1300 with depictions of saints, an early 16th-century tomb recess and Georgian box pews. Seventeenth-century communion rail. Several interesting monuments of 17th and 18th centuries, outstanding being that to Thomas Lewis, died 1747, by the sculptor Peter Scheemakers.

SOPLEY

Formerly in Hampshire, is now in Dorset.

➤ SOUTHAMPTON 421113

Holy Rood

October 1960

In the High Street which, when I first visited it by cycle one evening in 1946, was still suffering from the intense bombing raid of November 1940. Holy Rood Church had been wrecked, St Mary's with its steeple over to the east was a gutted shell, and only St Michael's of the town's original five stood more or less intact. Holy Rood had been mostly rebuilt in 1850, leaving some 14th-century walling in the chancel and tower. In 1957 the ruins were tidied up and dedicated as a memorial to Merchant Navy seamen. Tower no longer with a wooden spire but with its 'quarterjack' figures restored (their movements linked to the clock). Chancel subsequently re-roofed with glazing. Nave area left open, with large anchor a prominent feature. Portland stone fountain, a Titanic memorial of 1913 originally in cemetery on Southampton Common, and now accompanied by 'audioposts' giving commentaries.

v St Julien 419111

September 2018

In Winkle Street, off south end of High Street. Not a parish church, but historically the chapel of Domus Dei (God's House), founded late in 12th century as almshouse and travellers' hostel. Long used by French Protestants, hence the dedication. Basically the original building, with Transitional chancel arch, and in the chancel two piscinae. Much restored 1861, masking its antiquity, and tower made flat-topped. Not open to the public.

∨ St Mary 426116

September 2018

Six hundred yards east of the Bargate, in a large well treed churchyard. Completely rebuilt on a large scale by George Street, 1884. Gutted by bombing and again rebuilt 1954-56 by Romilly Craze, retaining Street's baptistry, magnificent steeple and parts of his outer walls, but castigated by Pevsner as a 'sadly squandered opportunity'. Closed for internal re-ordering at the time of writing. This was the St Mary's alluded to in the song 'The Bells of St Mary's' which picks up the rhythm of a peal.

∧ St Michael 419113

August 1946

To the west of the High Street and central to the old walled town, but miraculously spared in air raids. Saxon tower on massive arches, with shallow arcade over that facing nave. Upper part later, the slender stone spire heightened in 1732 as a landmark. Remainder of church largely 14th- to 15th-centuries, but with rather meagre arcades of 1828-29 designed for insertion of galleries, which were later removed. Square 12th-century font of black Tournai marble with dragons and angel carvings. Two 15th-century brass eagle lecterns, the finer one rescued from nearby Holy Rood Church. . Many monuments including tomb of Sir Richard Lyster, died 1552, with Gothic and Renaissance details intermingled.

⌄ SOUTH STONEHAM 440155

St Mary

August 1946

The village church of Swaythling, two miles north of Southampton. Chancel 12th-century with notable chancel arch – pointed and thus c.1190. Nave much altered 1854, with plain ceiling hiding medieval roof. South transept 1854 too. Small 15th-century tower. Small north transept housing large Baroque monument to Edward Dummer, died 1724. Many other memorials, including 16th-century tomb in chancel, canopied monument to Edmund Clarke, died 1632, with kneeling couple, and large tablet to Mary Jones, died 1828, made in Florence.

⌃ SOUTH HAYLING 722001

St Mary

August 1985

Unusual in being almost wholly of one period, mid-13th century, probably rebuilt on a new site following disastrous floods in 1324-25. Central tower and big shingled spire but no transepts. Arcade piers renewed in granite 1892 because of crumbling. These and the tower arches curious in that they spring about two feet above the capitals, from upward prolongations of the piers. Fine carved foliage and heads in the capitals. Medieval timber south porch. Square Purbeck marble font apparently older than the church. Some stained glass by Charles Kempe and a pupil.

△ SOUTH WARNBOROUGH 722472

St Andrew

October 1998

A little south of Odiham. 12th-century nave and 13th-century chancel. South aisle added by George Street, 1870, with glass screen of 2006. Roofs and bell-turret structure largely medieval, also the rood-loft, an unusual survival. But the chancel screen beneath it is by Street. Stained glass includes some 16th-century heraldry and on the north of the chancel a wartime London scene. Communion rail and lectern of 1950s by John Skelton. Chancel rather overfilled with monuments, many of them of 16th century to Whyte family.

▽ SOUTHWICK 627087

St James

August 1996

North-east of Fareham, behind Portsdown Hill. Rebuilt 1566, retaining some medieval walling and incorporating items from the former priory nearby. Irregular plan with unequal north arcade arches, no chancel arch, and low tower built within nave. Fascinating interior, little altered since the 18th century, with gallery on twisted wooden columns, 12th-century font, 'three-decker' pulpit, box pews in chancel, 17th-century altar table, 18th-century communion rail and panelling and, best of all, 18th-century reredos with classical surround to a painting of flying cherubs and doves. Painted Creed in gable over chancel entrance and benefaction boards at west end. Monuments include the canopied tomb of the 16th-century builder John Whyte with brasses depicting his family.

SPARSHOLT 435313

St Stephen

August 1993

Between Stockbridge and Winchester. Much altered 1882-83 by William Butterfield, including tower top, south porch, north arcade and aisle, and lengthening of the chancel. South arcade late Norman. Arches of chancel and tower 15th-century. Interesting south doorway (and door) of 1631. Chapel screen made from former 18th-century gallery.

STEVENTON 551472

St Nicholas

August 1994

Five miles east of Whitchurch. The church where Jane Austen's father was rector. Largely early 13th-century, but west front altered 1835, with new bell-turret and spire. Two ninth-century Cross-shafts with dragons and interlace ornament. Memorials to the Rev. James Austen (eldest brother of Jane), died 1819, and to Jane herself (died 1817, but tablet of 1936).

STEEP 745253

All Saints

June 1946

Just north of Petersfield. Largely early 13th-century in spite of misleadingly rendered exterior. Much restored and bell-turret rebuilt 1875-76. south arcade late 12th-century. Traceried 15th-century north door. Font of unusual hexagonal design 13th-century. Engraved window of 1978 to the local poet Edward Thomas by Laurence Whistler (copy of the vandalised original). Noteworthy set of embroidered hassocks.

⌄ STOCKBRIDGE 359350

St Peter

August 2005

Between Winchester and Salisbury. The old church, in a graveyard at the west end of the town, replaced 1866 by St Peter's in the High Street. Nave, aisles and south chapel demolished 1870, leaving the chancel of c.1200 with its arch blocked. Later west doorway, re-set. Some interesting fittings inside: altar table 1696; three-sided communion rail 17th-century; Royal arms 1726. Several wall-tablets, inside and out.

⌃ St Peter 355351

May 1946

The 'new' church of 1866 by John Colson in the High Street. His prominent tower and spire were added in 1887. Some 14th-century stonework transferred here, also the square 12th-century Purbeck marble font. Of the stained glass the best is early 20th-century, by J. Powell and Sons.

119

⌄ STOKE CHARITY   488393

St Michael

March 1966

Six miles north of Winchester. No village around it, just the Norman church in a field. Nave, north aisle and north chapel. The north aisle was once the nave of a Saxon church. Its two arches and enormous pier are early 11th-century, but the splendid chancel arch is of 1180 and so is the little doorway next to it. Chancel 13th-century. Nave 14th-century with bell-turret and plain doorway. Its roof probably 17th-century. North chapel late 15th-century with an unusually bold frieze to its roof. Font 12th-century. Interesting floor tiles, piscina and fragmentary wall-paintings and 15th-century glass. Found embedded in the nave wall and now on a bracket, a fine sculpture of the Mass of St Gregory, c.1500. Exceptionally good collection of 12th- to 17th-century monuments, mostly to Hampton family: no fewer than six tomb-chests, some with brasses and mostly with effigies. More 18th-century tombs and headstones in churchyard.

⌃ STRATFIELD SAYE   695614

St Mary

July 2009

Eight miles north-east of Basingstoke on the Loddon. Church in park by river rebuilt in brick 1754-58 by John Pitt for his father Lord Rivers, on a site further from the house. Cruciform, attractively whitened outside, with copper roofs and octagonal dome. Early 18th-century box pews and 'two-decker' pulpit. Barrel organ with 'Gothick' case. Other furnishings relatively modern. A variety of memorials to Pitt family and others, from 16th to 20th centuries and rich with heraldry. Notable are a tablet by Eric Gill to Lord Richard Wellesley, died 1914, and less seriously in the porch an epitaph to John Baylie, died 1777, 'unofficial jester' to Lord Rivers: '… his only sin was a drop of gin'.

SYDMONTON 484579

St Mary

May 1999

Six miles south of Newbury. Entirely rebuilt 1853 by J.P. Harrison. Norman doorways, also chancel arch reinstated as tower arch. Deconsecrated, on the lawn of a private estate and converted internally into a small theatre.

STRATFIELD TURGIS 690600

All Saints

October 1998

North-east of Basingstoke, on the bank of the Loddon. Declared redundant 1969, stripped of fittings and sadly left to deteriorate. Roof repaired but windows boarded up. Thirteenth-century nave. Bell-turret 1899. Chancel rebuilt in brick 1792 after a fire.

⌄ TADLEY 597599

St Peter

January 2003

Five miles north-west of Basingstoke. Much altered over the centuries, especially about 1600, and typical of Hampshire. South porch 1689 brick, but doorway 15th-century. Brick tower possibly of 1685. Nice west gallery and stair 17th-century – also altar table, communion rail and pulpit.

⌃ TANGLEY 335524

St Thomas of Canterbury

August 2009

Six miles north-west of Andover, on the Roman road from Winchester. Extensively rebuilt 1875 by William White. Tower by him 1897. Apse rebuilt on Norman foundations. Curious twin Norman window above, probably not where it was. Cylindrical lead font thought to be 17th-century, with roses, fleurs-de-lys and thistles.

THRUXTON 289456

SS Peter and Paul

May 1999

Four miles west of Andover on A303. Nearly hidden by trees in summer, rather limiting possible viewpoints! Much altered in the 1840s and 1860s. Tower rebuilt 1801-02 re-using interesting carved stones from a demolished early 16th-century north chapel. From that still stands the tomb of Sir John Lewis and his wife (both died 1524) in an elaborate arched surround opening into the present vestry (1839). Moreover there was once a south chapel alongside the chancel as well, and this only survives to the extent of the ornately recessed tomb of Sir Nicholas Lisle (died 1506), its arch curiously altered in 1869 to allow for a window and doorway. Many 19th-century furnishings, including the rich altarpiece, font and cover, patterned tiles and painted texts. The texts, and the best of the stained glass, are by Thomas Willement. Knight's effigy of c.1200 under the tower, the earliest in Hampshire. Big brass effigy of an earlier Sir John Lisle (died 1407) in chancel floor. Rare oak effigy of Elizabeth Philpott (died 1616).

TICHBORNE 568303

St Andrew

July 1946

Just south-west of New Alresford. Chancel early Norman, with typical pilaster strips on east gable but 14th-century east window below. Nave and arcades 13th-century. Brick tower of 1703. Font 12th-century. Box pews and communion rail early 17th-century. North chapel most unusual in being still Roman Catholic, railed off and with monuments to Tichborne family – notably Sir Benjamin (died 1629).

◀ TIMSBURY 345245

St Andrew

March 1993

Close to the north of Romsey. Mostly 13th-century, with unspoilt interior. A few bits of 15th-century glass in chancel windows. Screen 15th-century, plain and rustic. Jacobean panel at back of pulpit.

▼ TITCHFIELD 541057

St Peter

June 1959

Two miles west of Fareham. Prominent tower, considered in its lower part to be ninth- or even eighth-century, and still acting as a porch. Traces of high Saxon roof lines on its sides. Twelfth-century inner doorway with zigzag ornament. Twelfth-century south arcade and aisle replaced 1867. Large north aisle 16th-century with a stately arcade and a degree of elaboration unusual in Hampshire. South chapel with its arcade 14th-century: amusing fanciful creatures and foliage in the capitals. Interesting wall-painting of Miraculous Draught of Fishes on west wall. Crucifixion painting over chancel arch by Charles Kempe, 1889. Majestic late 16th-century monument in south chapel to Earls of Southampton, with three recumbent effigies in two tiers. The family's riches came from the spoliation of Hampshire monasteries, not least Titchfield Abbey itself. Amongst the less ostentatious memorials is one to Mary Wriothesley (died 1615 aged four), attributed to the sculptor Epiphanius Evesham.

⌄ TUFTON 458468

St Mary

August 2003

Just south of Whitchurch. Nave and narrow chancel arch early Norman, with big domestic-looking windows inserted on each side. Chancel 13th-century with lancet windows set in neat arcading. Exceptionally big wall-painting of St Christopher 15th-century.

⌃ TUNWORTH 673484

All Saints

February 2002

Three miles south-east of Basingstoke. Nave, chancel and bell-turret rebuilt 1854-55, probably by Henry Woodyer and to old plan, incorporating pointed chancel arch of c.1200, south doorway of c.1300 and stonework of two small windows. Alms-box called 'funny and engaging' by Pevsner, probably Victorian.

▼ UPHAM 538206

No dedication

June 1946

A little north-west of Bishops Waltham. Eighteenth-century brick tower. Otherwise entirely rebuilt by George Street, 1881. North and south arcades differ for no obvious reason. A 13th-century arch at east end of north aisle.

▲ TWYFORD 481251

St Mary

September 1967

On the Itchen south of Winchester. Rebuilt 1876-77 by Alfred Waterhouse. Late 12th-century piers of previous church re-used, but otherwise in a sort of Perpendicular style. Memorials by two celebrated sculptors – to Jonathan Shipley, died 1788, by Nollekens, and to Shipley's daughter Georgiana, died 1806, by Flaxman.

ⱽ UP NATELY   701519

St Stephen

October 1956

On A30, east of Basingstoke. A name for new parents to identify with! Norman chancel arch and north doorway. Banded flint and brick facings externally, apparently of 1844. But all nicely unrestored inside, with 16th-century roof, early 18th-century communion rail and lead poor box with painted cherub.

ⱔ UPPER CLATFORD   357435

All Saints

August 1996

Close to the south of Andover, on the Anton. Extremely unusual in having wood posts down the centre of the nave. What appears to be a double chancel arch is in fact two bays of the 12th-century former north arcade, re-set here in the 17th century and necessitating the wide spread of the roof overall. The actual chancel was extended in 1890-91. Brick porch perhaps 17th-century, with glazed outer doors of 2004 embellished with 'trout' handles. Tower base 14th-century, but upper part bears date 1576. Font of baluster form 1629, with curious cover. Good early 17th-century pulpit. Large hall added to north-east by Clive Spencer, 1998.

⌄ UPPER ELDON 365278

St John the Baptist

August 1993

Four miles north of Romsey. In the care of Churches Conservation Trust. A tiny late 12th-century building in the grounds of a farmhouse. Remarkable for survival of nine recesses for consecration crosses of that date. East wall rebuilt in brick 1729. Plain interior with open roof.

⌃ UPTON GREY 697485

St Mary

August 1997

Four miles south-east of Basingstoke. A complex church architecturally, with the central tower and crossing 'much pulled about' to quote Pevsner. Nave curiously short, with 12th-century arch to tower, and blocked arches to former early 13th-century south aisle. Then a lower arch to the long, mainly 13th-century chancel. Brick north aisle of 1715, spacious but with a rather nondescript set of round arches. Small 16th-century font with 17th-century cover. Numerous smaller monuments, notably the tablets to Dorothy Eyre, died 1650, and John Matthew, died 1689. In the churchyard a strange granite memorial to Charles Holmes, died 1924, with very mannered lettering.

⚐ VERNHAM DEAN 349570

St Mary

September 1999

On the Wiltshire border north of Andover, prettily situated in a valley. Parts are 13th-century, but much is from 'restorations' of 1700 and 1851-52. Rather naïve stained glass of the latter period, regarded by Pevsner as 'very lovable'. West doorway a fine example of the transition from Norman to Early English.

⚐ WARBLINGTON 728054

St Thomas à Becket

May 1971

Very near the south-east of Havant, yet amongst tall trees and farmland. Long sloping roofs to protect from sea gales, around a central tower proved to be basically Saxon. This is much like Titchfield's, but with the bottom parts opened out and a third storey added in the 13th century (the spire is 19th-century). North arcade with pointed arches probably late 12th-century. South arcade 13th century, much more advanced, with detached Purbeck marble shafts against the piers. Long chancel later 13th-century. Fourteenth-century north porch with interesting robust woodwork. Two worn medieval effigies in recesses, and several good wall-tablets of the Georgian period. In the churchyard some well-carved tombstones: one to north of tower depicts H.M.S. *Torbay* burning in Portsmouth Harbour in 1758. Also two early 19th-century brick huts used by watchmen against body-snatchers.

⌄ WARNFORD   623226

Our Lady

June 1946

In a park astride the Meon, midway between Winchester and Petersfield. Asserted by a 12th-century inscription to have been founded in the seventh century by St Wilfrid of York. Another inscription on a south porch sundial may indeed be seventh-century. Rather forbidding tower late 12th-century. Nave and chancel (without a chancel arch) early 13th-century but with east window displaying 14th-century tracery. Square 12th-century font. Chancel screen 17th-century, and probably tower screen too. Plain 16th-century seating, also three 15th-century stalls now by the south wall. Eighteenth-century communion rail. Seventeenth-century monuments to Neale family, one with three effigies as though on shelves.

⌄ WEEKE   468306

St Matthew

August 1943

In the west suburb of Winchester, on the Stockbridge Road. Nave early 12th-century, with 15th-century roof timbers. Chancel and its arch 13th-century. Windows mostly altered in 17th century. Bell-turret and vestry 19th-century. Some minor monuments – among them a brass of 1498 high on the north wall, depicting St Christopher.

⌄ WEST MEON   640242

St John Evangelist

February 2007

In the Meon valley six miles west of Petersfield. Entirely rebuilt 1843-45 by George Gilbert Scott in sober Early English style. Delicately carved Royal arms of Queen Anne.

⌃ WEST TISTED   650293

St Mary Magdalen

May 1992

Between A31, A32 and A272, by the site of a demolished manor house. Nave early 12th-century, but chancel mostly of 1848. Brick porch 18th-century. Font plain 13th-century.

131

⌄ WEST TYTHERLEY 274297

April 2000

Rebuilt in brick 1833 by G. Guthrie. Still classical but windows made Gothic and stone chancel added 1877. Square font probably 13th-century. Brass of 1480 to a lady.

⌃ WEST WORLDHAM 741370

St Nicholas

November 2000

Two miles south-east of Alton. Probably early 13th-century, but rescued from a roofless ruin 1888. In the west window two little 17th-century heraldic panels.

⌄ WEYHILL 318465

St Michael

April 1958

Three miles west of Andover. Norman chancel arch. Chancel Early English in style but much rebuilt by J.H. Hakewill 1862-3, along with added south arcade and aisle and general renewal of external flintwork. Nave roof timbers believed to date from 1506. Bell-turret 1907. Several windows of around 1900 and one of 1937 by Ninian Comper. Two carved grave stones of the 11th century. Later memorials include a fine one by Sir Richard Westmacott to John Gawler, 1803.

⌃ WESTON PATRICK 69146

St Laurence

August 1997

Four miles south-east of Basingstoke. Completely rebuilt 1866-68 by Thomas Wyatt, who was lord of the manor. Twelfth-century north doorway retained. Interior dominated by wooden chancel arch – like the bell-turret, an invention of Wyatt's.

⅄ WHERWELL 391408

St Peter and Holy Cross

June 2018

South-east of Andover, on the Test, close to the site of a nuns' abbey. The pronunciation 'Hurrell' is less tongue-tying. Church totally rebuilt 1854-58 by Henry Woodyer with his somewhat idiosyncratic window tracery and spiky bell-turret. A collection of carved stone inside, mostly from the monastery church and including a 13th-century depiction of the Harrowing of Hell. Engraved 'Millennium' window by Tony Gilliam in south aisle, contrasting with the 19th-century stained glass elsewhere. In the churchyard the large mausoleum of the Iremonger family, incorporating some more medieval fragments.

⅄ WHITCHURCH 460477

All Hallows

June 1949

On the Test, with a conspicuous tower and spire by Benjamin Ferrey 1867-68, built on a 13th-century base. South arcade also 13th-century, but north arcade 15th-century. Aisles widened by Ferrey and east bays rebuilt, but west part of nave roof is 15th-century, and so is a wooden stair in the tower, an uncommon survivor. Font 15th-century too. Fascinating painted panel naïvely illustrating the Ten Commandments, dated 1602. Outstandingly important ninth-century gravestone with demi-figure of Christ in arched recess, a memorial to one Frithburh. Other monuments include two to the paper-making Portal family.

⚐ WHITSBURY 129192

St Leonard

October 2006

On the Wiltshire boundary five miles north of Fordingbridge. A 13th-century hilltop church entirely rebuilt in 1878, with brick tower and simple interior.

⚐ WICKHAM 576114

St Nicholas

November 2006

In the Meon valley north of Fareham, prominently on a possibly prehistoric mound. Nave, chancel, transepts and west tower. South transept brick. Tower of the 1860s by F. and H. Francis, with 12th-century doorway re-set. Monuments include the canopied tomb of Sir William Uvedale, 1615, with family effigies and bristling with emblems of mortality.

⋎ WIDLEY 668066

Christ

November 2006

On Portsdown Hill north of Portsmouth. The medieval church of St Mary Magdalene stood in open country to the north-west and was demolished in the 1950s leaving the graveyard with a few headstones (SU 659074). Christ Church Portsdown, amongst trees at the top of the hill on the old A3 road, superseded it in 1874. By John Colson, a version of Norman in style. Good series of stained glass aisle windows of 1950s by Michael Farrar-Bell, together with west window of 1948 by Reginald Bell commemorating meeting by 2nd Army H.Q. Staff in the church on the eve of D-Day.

⋏ WIELD 628387

St James

July 1995

Five miles west of Alton. Nave and chancel 12th-century with simple doorways and 15th-century windows. East wall rebuilt in 1880s. Bellcote 1812. Modest interior with traces of 13th-century wall-paintings. Square Norman font found in a garden in Winchester. Royal arms of Queen Anne over chancel arch. Fine alabaster monument to Sir William Wallope and a tablet to Barbara Willys, both died 1617.

WINCHESTER

The Cathedral is outside the scope of this book of parish churches. So are the splendid chapel of Winchester College, the chapel of St John's Hospital (which served for many years as a boys' school) and the Bishops' Chapel of Wolvesey College. Nor, as elsewhere in the county, are the parishes newly formed in the 19th and 20th centuries included. With the very notable exception of St Cross, which is outside the city proper, the churches are all of relatively minor interest.

❯ St Bartholomew 482302

August 1943

The church of Hyde. Twelfth-century south wall and doorway and east bays of north arcade. Tower of 1541, of stone from demolished Hyde Abbey. Remainder much altered and rebuilt in 19th century (chancel and north chapel 1859). Some elaborate early 20th-century woodwork in pulpit, altar etc. Interesting 12th-century carved stones, also from the abbey – animals and foliage.

∨   St Cross   476277

August 1993

I include the church of the Hospital of St Cross (with a black-and-white reproduction of a water-colour) because it has served the parish of St Faith since 1507, when that church was demolished. The Hospital was founded about 1130, not to provide medical care in the modern sense of the word, but to give poor men food and lodging – a tradition that still survives there in a little-altered form. Looking not unlike a smaller version of the Cathedral, the church embodies the finest design and craftsmanship of, primarily, 1160 to 1250, and thus covers the period when Norman Romanesque round arches gave way to Gothic pointed.

The choir was built first, then the transepts and the eastern bay of the short nave, then the rest of the nave with the north porch by about 1250. The nave clerestory is mid-14th-century, but its vault was not finished till the early 15th century. The central tower was raised and the roofs of the choir and transepts re-formed with vaults later in the 14th century. That is a much simplified account of a complex structure which resulted from over two

centuries of development, yet is remarkable for its unity. William Butterfield made many mainly superficial changes in 1844-65.

Amongst the furnishings and fittings the following should certainly be noted: medieval floor tiles in and around the east end; remnants of early 16th-century choir stalls; fine 16th-century stone screens; a little 15th-century glass; 12th-century and later wall-paintings in the east chapels and elsewhere; ingenious early 17th-century communion rails in south-east chapel; 16th-century bench-ends in north transept; square 12th-century font from St Faith's; eagle lectern with parrot's head (not ancient but copied from one in a Cheshire church).

- St John the Baptist   487295

May 2009

Over the Itchen, below St Giles' Hill. Arcades late 12th-century 'Transitional'. Aisles widened in 13th-century, with noteworthy Geometric tracery at south-east. Tower late 14th-century, like most of the timber roofs. Some 13th-century wall-paintings at west end. Fifteenth-century rood screen right across interior, with stair in turret in south wall. Fourteenth-century parclose screens to chapels. Fifteenth-century font. Sixteenth-century wooden pulpit. Chandelier probably 18th-century. Tomb-chest in north chapel probably served as Easter sepulchre. Some 18th-century memorial tablets.

- St Lawrence   482295

August 1943

As the sketch suggests, completely hemmed in by other buildings in The Square and High Street. Now just a plain rectangle with attached 15th-century tower, but 12th-century north wall said to be part of the Conqueror's palace where Domesday Book was written. Largely rebuilt in 17th century after use as a school. Damaged by fire in the 1970s and restored. Little else of interest except 17th-century bells and a few wall-tablets.

- St Maurice   481295

August 1943

Once a collegiate church but now merely represented by its 15th-century tower. The nave of 1842 glimpsed in the sketch was demolished in 1958. Good 12th-century doorway with zigzag ornament.

- St Michael   481280

August 1943

Thirteenth-century tower with 15th-century top. North arcade and aisle removed 1822, and the whole space roofed over. Remainder much rebuilt by Butterfield 1879-82, with his typically ornate tiling. Font probably 16th-century. Many small memorials from 17th century onwards.

➤ St Swithun-upon-Kingsgate 482291

August 1943

Literally over the 14th-century city gateway, and reached by a 16th-century roofed stair. Little of medieval work left after successive 'restorations', apart from the roof. Windows mostly of Tudor domestic character. Fifteenth-century font let into west wall to gain space. A few small monuments, including a 1622 brass depicting in their shrouds the four children of John Bond.

⊿ St Peter Chesil 486290

August 1943

Deconsecrated, and converted in 1963 for use by a theatre club, but hardly changed externally. Of remarkably irregular plan, with three arches of south arcade all of different sizes. Probably there was a north arcade, removed in medieval times to make a wider nave – which still has a 14th-century roof. South aisle now partitioned but with a 13th-century roof.

➤ St Thomas 478293

August 1943

Deconsecrated, and now split into offices. Completely rebuilt 1845-57 by the relatively unknown architect E.W. Elmslie. The 180-foot spire is prominent in views of the city. Pevsner praised 'the ensemble as well as the details'.

⩔ WINCHFIELD 767536

St Mary

October 1956

Two miles north-east of Odiham. An outstanding Norman church, documented as completed by 1150. West tower, nave and chancel. North aisle added 1849-50 by Henry Woodyer, and top of tower rebuilt. Spectacular chancel arch with curious pattern of rolls on its underside, as well as the normal zigzag ornament, here all exceptionally rich and still wonderfully clear-cut. South doorway equally splendid, within a 15th-century porch. Simpler north doorway with pointed arch. North and south windows of chancel with ornament similar to chancel arch. Plain 12th-century font. Pulpit dated 1634, and communion rail of similar date. Fine 'Annunciation' west window by Herbert Hendrie, early 20th-century 'Arts and Crafts'. Engraved south window 'Tree of Life' by Laurence Whistler, 1978.

⩔ WINNALL 491300

St Martin

August 1943

In a north-east suburb of Winchester. Completely rebuilt 1858 by William Coles, with some old stonework re-used. Demolished in the 1960s. Some wall-tablets are now in St John's, Winchester.

WOLVERTON 552586

St Catherine

March 1957

Two miles east of Kingsclere. Rebuilt in brick 1717 by an unknown architect. Nave, chancel, transepts, and big tower with stone dressings. Interestingly shaped gables. Large plain chancel arch with smaller side arches, turned to allow access to pulpit and reading desk. Windows foolishly subdivided with brick mullions by the Victorian restorer who evidently couldn't bear a church without at least a hint of Gothic – and for good measure swept away a west gallery. Excellent fittings and furnishings otherwise, contemporary with the church and including box pews, wall-panelling, reredos with marquetry, wrought-iron communion rail, 'baluster' font, and chancel floor with inlaid marble. Good Royal arms of 1846.

WINSLADE 654481

St Mary

February 2002

South of Basingstoke on the Alton road. Deconsecrated. Converted into a dwelling 2007. Chancel and south wall of nave substantially 13th-century. Yellow brick tower 1816. Otherwise mostly of 1876.

⋎ WONSTON 476395

Holy Trinity

March 1960

Six miles north of Winchester. Late 12th-century south dooway and pointed chancel arch. Chancel early 13th-century with later east window. Tower early 16th-century with 17th-century wicket door. North aisle added 1829, but arcade rebuilt 40 years later. Some good early 20th-century glass, particularly in the side windows of the chancel, by Morris and Co.

⋏ WOODCOTT 433548

St James

August 2003

Five miles north of Whitchurch, a mile or so west of A34. Rebuilt 1704, and again completely in 1853. Some interesting carved work of unknown foreign origin in pulpit and reading desk.

❧ WOOTTON ST LAWRENCE   592532

St Lawrence

June 1949

Three miles west of Basingstoke. A church of early origin over-enthusiastically 'restored' by John Colson in 1864. Three bays of north arcade 12th-century (but rebuilt), with west bay added a little later. Showy south arcade wholly Colson's. Chancel also rebuilt, but with some window stonework re-used. Tower 15th-century with roof by Colson. Fine Royal arms of George IV. Engraved glass in south window by Laurence Whistler, 1990, a contrast to the dark stained glass in the others. Excellent monument to Sir Thomas Hooke, died 1677, with semi-reclining figure. Tablet to William Wither, died 1733, believed to be by Roubiliac. In the floor many 17th- and 18th-century ledger stones worth examining for their fine incised lettering.

❧ WORTING   601518

St Thomas of Canterbury

October 1960

A little west of Basingstoke, in a village not quite swamped by its expanded neighbour. Rebuilt 1847-48 by Henry Woodyer on old foundations. The decoration of the chancel ceiling and of the 1873 organ case deserves attention.

⌄ WYMERING 651057

SS Peter and Paul

October 1960

North of Portsmouth on the mainland. Externally much rebuilt by George Street 1860-61. Arcades late 12th-century (north) and early 13th-century (south), the latter with the oddity of columns rising above the capitals before the start of the arches. That is rather like South Hayling. Good 19th-century glass in east window, and below it a richly carved three-panelled reredos.

⌃ YATELEY 817609

St Peter

May 1942

On the Berkshire border, south of Wokingham. My second-ever Hampshire church, in 1942, alas severely damaged by arson in 1979. To a great extent restored (a gratifying amount of the ancient woodwork having survived), and added to on the south. Nave basically 11th-century on the north side, with a Sarsen stone just east of the 14th-century north porch, suggesting a very early origin. North doorway 12th-century and chancel 13th-century. Wooden tower late 15th-century with internal 'aisles' on three sides between the supporting posts. Brick infilling restored 1878. A few 16th-century memorial brasses. Some interesting headstones in churchyard, and a much renewed 17th-century revolving lychgate.